THE RESURRECTION OF THE DEAD CITIES

MICHAEL SCANTLEBURY

THE RESURRECTION OF THE DEAD ONES
Copyright © 2025 by Michael Scantlebury

Editorial Consultant: Anita Thompson – 604-521-6042

All rights reserved. Neither this publication nor any part of this publication may be reproduced or transmitted in any form or by any means, electronic or mechanical, including photocopying, recording or any information storage and retrieval system, without permission in writing from the author.

All Scripture quotations, unless otherwise indicated, are taken from the Revised Standard Version. Copyright © 1946, 1952, and 1971 the Division of Christian Education of the National Council of the Churches of Christ in the United States of America. Used by permission. All rights reserved. All Scriptures marked KJV are taken from the King James Version; all marked NIV are from The New International Version; and those marked MSG are from The Message Bible and is used by permission.

Hebrew and Greek definitions are from James Strong, Strong's Exhaustive Concordance of the Bible (Peabody, MA: Hendrickson Publishers, n.d.).

Michael Scantlebury has taken author's prerogative in capitalizing certain words that are not usually capitalized according to standard grammatical practice. Also, please note that the name satan and related names are not capitalized as we choose not to acknowledge him, even to the point of disregarding standard grammatical practice.

ISBN: Softcover: 978-1-4866-2737-0
eBook ISBN: 978-1-4866-2738-7

Word Alive Press
119 De Baets Street Winnipeg, MB R2J 3R9
www.wordalivepress.ca

Cataloguing in Publication information is can be obtained from Library and Archives Canada.

Other Books by Michael Scantlebury

Navigating Through Spiritual Transitions
Exploring the Secrets of Hidden Wealth
God's Eternal Plan
Understanding the Both Sides of Faith
Understanding the Revelation – An In-Depth Study
Are We Living in The End Times or The Last Days?
Fathers and Sons – An Unveiling
Heaven and Earth – A Biblical Understanding
My Ponderings
Understanding the Kingdom of God and The Church of Jesus Christ
Eschatology – A Biblical View
As It Was in the Beginning, So Shall It Be…
Daniel In Babylon – The Study Guide
Principles for Victorious Living Volume II
Principles for Victorious Living Volume I
Present Truth Lifestyle – Daniel In Babylon
Esther: Present Truth Church
The Fortress Church
Called to be An Apostle – An Autobiography
Leaven Revealed
Five Pillars of The Apostolic
Apostolic Purity
Apostolic Reformation
Jesus Christ The Apostle and High Priest of Our Profession
Kingdom Advancing Prayer Volume I
Kingdom Advancing Prayer Volume II
Kingdom Advancing Prayer Volume III
Internal Reformation
God's Nature Expressed Through His Names
"I Will Build My Church." – Jesus Christ

Contents

CHAPTER ONE
UNDERSTANDING THE BIBLE — 1

CHAPTER TWO
AN IMPORTANT QUESTION — 23

CHAPTER THREE
THE SECOND COMING AND ETERNAL LIFE OR WHERE ARE THE DEAD? — 29

CHAPTER FOUR
DANIEL ON THE RESURRECTION — 49

CHAPTER FIVE
THE LAST TRUMPET — 67

CHAPTER SIX
UNDERSTANDING THE RESURRECTION OF THE DEAD ONES — 77

OTHER EXCITING TITLES — 101

"And as it is appointed for men to die once, but after this the judgment," Hebrews 9:2

CHAPTER ONE
UNDERSTANDING THE BIBLE

What happens to a person when they die? It is one of the most asked and least understood questions in all of life and for the Christian, it entails the idea of a resurrection. Every Christian denomination—and there are many—believe one simple truth: the tomb was empty after the crucifixion of Jesus. We often hear sermons where the focus is on the cross and the resurrection is mentioned only in passing. But when you really get into the meat of the word of God, the Bible clearly shows that the resurrection of Jesus was the gospel message preached by the Apostles and not the cross.

Sadly, the Believers only seem to get excited about the resurrection once a year at Easter time. In reality, every Sunday should be Resurrection Sunday. The early Church met on the first day of the week to celebrate Jesus' defeat of death. Imagine the impact from consciously gathering every week to celebrate the resurrection.

And in that vein, we need to seek to arrive at a clear biblical understanding of this particular question regarding what happens to a person when they die. It is my earnest prayer that we, together, could arrive at a much better understanding of this subject. And before going any further let me say this: of course I do not have all the answers as I have not died and been resurrected, but I will seek to address this subject with as much clarity as can be gleaned from Scripture and do hope that you would benefit from the truths uncovered therein.

However, before going into the 'meat' of this book, please allow me to say this with regards to the creation of mankind:

Psalm 90:10 tells us:

The days of our lives are seventy years; And if by reason of strength they are eighty years, Yet their boast is only labor and sorrow; For it is soon cut off, and we fly away.

This verse caused me to revisit the creation of the first human couple. Never saw this in this light before—Adam, and **NOT** Eve was created in Eden and then God chose a place in Eden and named it, The Garden of Eden and there He placed Adam [It is like we are living/created here in British Columbia [BC], but after we were created we were then placed in Vancouver to live. We are still in BC, but we are specifically in Vancouver. I hope you understand this] <u>and then God created Eve.</u>

This Garden in the original Hebrew text meant that it was a protected place. This was done because God knew what they would eventually do and as such needed to have this place protected.

Let us revisit the account in Genesis 2:7-8, 15-23

And the Lord God formed man of the dust of the ground, and breathed into his nostrils the breath of life; and man became a living being. The Lord God planted a garden eastward in Eden, and there He put the man whom He had formed.

*Then the Lord God took the man and put him in the garden of Eden to tend and keep it. [***At this point Eve was not yet created***] And the Lord God commanded the man, [Adam, and not Eve, as she was not yet created] saying, "Of every tree of the garden you may freely eat; but of the tree of the knowledge of good and evil you shall not eat, for in the day that you eat of it you shall surely die." And the Lord God said, "It is not good that man should be alone; I will make him a helper comparable to him." Out of the ground the Lord God formed every beast of the field and every bird of the air, and brought them to Adam to see what he would call them. And whatever Adam called each living creature, that was its name. So Adam gave names to all cattle, to the birds of the air, and to every beast of the field [***Here we see Adam doing all the initial work***

of naming all the animals God had created]. *But for Adam there was not found a helper comparable to him.* [**Now, the creation of Eve, in the protected realm of The Garden of Eden.**] *And the Lord God caused a deep sleep to fall on Adam, and he slept; and He took one of his ribs, and closed up the flesh in its place. Then the rib which the Lord God had taken from man He made into a woman, and He brought her to the man. And Adam said: "This is now bone of my bones And flesh of my flesh; She shall be called Woman, Because she was taken out of Man."* (Emphasis and Parenthesis Author's)

Now, remember that it was into the first man Adam, God breathed His breath into and he became alive with all his learning/information to live successfully. However, they sinned after Eve was created.

Now we have to understand and see how crafty the devil was/is, he first tempted Eve as I do believe that he knew that God did not specifically speak to her, nor did He initially breathe His Spirit into her but into the man Adam. So he decided that she would be tempted first and then he would let her get her husband to follow her and disobey God.

[Eve first sinned and I do believe that if Adam had not heeded to the voice of his wife, God's plan would have been altered, because it was into Adam God breathed and not directly into Eve. I believe she got God's Breath from the rib of Adam. So, Adam had to be enticed to also eat of that forbidden fruit—Genesis 3:17] by disobeying God and to be kicked out of that protected realm; The Garden of Eden and a flaming sword was set up to guard that protected realm.

Let us see it again in the following passage:
Genesis 3:22-24

Then the Lord God said, "Behold, the man has become like one of Us, to know good and evil. And now, lest he put out his hand and take also of the tree of life, and eat, and live forever"—therefore the Lord God sent him out of the garden of Eden to till the ground from which he was taken. So He drove out the man; [**and in reality the woman as well**] *and He placed cherubim at the east of the garden of Eden, and a flaming sword which turned every way, to guard the way to the tree of life.* (Emphasis and Parenthesis Author's)

And as we all know death was introduced. As a matter, I do believe that death was introduced as an act of Mercy on God's part. Mankind had to be able to die so that God's plan of redemption could be implemented.

In the early days of earth man used to live very long, but their sinful lifestyle got worse and worse until God just could not take it anymore so He wiped out His creation and started over with Noah and his family. Eight souls to be exact and we began to see the life span of humans lessen.

No matter what life form it is, it must be connected to a source or it will quickly cease to exist.

However, as I have shared before, let me share it again by way of a reminder, when it comes to humans, both male and female, they too must be connected to their Source in order to survive. We need earth because all of natural life is connected here, no matter what kind of life we are referring to. All plant and animal life is connected to the earth. Whether birds or animals or plants once within the earth's gravitational pull, MUST BE connected to the earth in order to survive.

However when we come to humankind we have two sources; earth for our natural sustenance and earthly survival. But we were also connected to a Heavenly Source in our Creator God, Who breathed His Breath into us through Adam, (and as such, the first human couple lived through their Source by God's Spirit being alive in them). However, once they (Adam and Eve) cut themselves off from this vital and absolutely needed source, their source from earth only allowed them to live so long, their death from the Spiritual source soon manifested in their natural death, which has been shortened through time.

That is why we MUST BE BORN-AGAIN, born from ABOVE! And be given eternal life. HALLELUJAH, our God is truly the Master Genius, what a brilliant plan. Once we exit this earth realm and leave this connection we will be in His Presence and would live eternally in His Presence. This is what Jesus did for us through His Birth, Death and His Resurrection. Then giving us the great gift of Eternal Life, through Salvation in His Name!

EXCITING WE WILL NOT DIE, EVER AGAIN! That is the ultimate prize for living a righteous life, here and NOW!

Also please note that this book will take on somewhat of a "classroom" atmosphere, as facts cannot be presented in any other way when we seek together to arrive at a biblical understanding of this all-important issue of death and resurrection.

So, here we go…

HOW DO WE INTERPRET SCRIPTURE?

Some people practice reading the Scriptures as follows: they open the book with eyes closed, point to a portion of Scripture and wherever they land, that is the relevant, inspired word of God for them for the day, regardless of who the Scripture was meant for, when it was written, and in what context it was written in. This is a spiritual type of Russian roulette, about as accurate as your daily horoscope and can cause wavering off the path intended by the Lord for us to follow. "Audience Relevance" or understanding the audience when Scripture was being written is very vital if we are to grasp the full meaning of all that was written. That is how we interpret the Scripture!

The subject of audience relevance is very vital and this may perhaps shock many people, but there is not one book in the entire Bible that was written **TO** anyone living today. Every single book in the Bible was written **FOR** us for application and understanding, but none of them were written TO us. Here is what the writer of 2 Timothy tells us: 2 Timothy 3:16-17

> *All Scripture is given by inspiration of God, and is profitable **FOR** doctrine, **FOR** reproof, **FOR** correction, **FOR** instruction in righteousness, that the man of God may be complete, thoroughly equipped **FOR** every good work.* (Emphasis Author's)

Every book in the Bible is a personal letter, a history book, or writing by a Prophet or an Apostle to a particular people at a particular time and for a particular reason. Yes, we do glean truth and understanding from these books today, but that is far different than saying that these books were written **TO** us. To put it another way, we are reading their mail. If someone in the present day happens to say, "Here's what this Scripture means to me," the reality is such that it doesn't matter what it means to that person. It only matters what it meant to the original audience. Few of us stand up and say this. We let the more mystical aspect of the feelings infiltrate our Bible study, which is not what God intended.

That is where we find out what the Bible truly means, and at this point, we then can apply it to ourselves. Otherwise, it is all open to interpretation and the readers will see things within the Scriptures which are not actually there. We cannot mold the Word of God to fit into that which we desire it to say. You may have heard the illustration about the person who read the Bible in said manner. They opened up the Bible and the Scripture verse of the day was *"And Judas hanged himself"*. They followed in the same vein for another Scripture and the one that appeared was *"go thou and do likewise."* Yes, this is somewhat in jest, but it illustrates the folly of this type of Bible study where a lone verse or two of Scripture pulled out of a hat should never be the mode for studying the Scriptures.

Again, as we read, let us remember the context of the following passage. It was written in the 1st Century at the beginning of the New Testament Church and spoken to Old Testament Saints, who were newly converted to this *"New Way"* and who for the most part understood that when a person died they really went to "sleep" to be eventually awakened at the resurrection. So here in this passage the *[Apostle]* Paul is bringing them new converts up to speed on some things as it pertained to the resurrection.

> *For we know that if our earthly house, this tent, is destroyed, we have a building from God, a house not made with hands, eternal in the heavens. For in this we groan, earnestly desiring to be clothed with our habitation which is from heaven, if indeed, having been clothed, we shall not be found naked. For we who are in this tent groan, being burdened, not because we want to be unclothed, but further clothed, that mortality may be swallowed up by life. Now He who has prepared us for this very thing is God, who also has given us the Spirit as a guarantee. So we are always confident, knowing that while we are at home in the body we are absent from the Lord. For we walk by faith, not by sight. We are confident, yes, well pleased rather to be absent from the body and to be present with the Lord.* (2 Corinthians 5:1-8)

So, as we go further into this writing, one thing we would like to remember which is paramount is that these Scriptures were written in the 1st Century before the Old Covenant Temple [God's dwelling place] was destroyed. They were living in what can be best described as the "crossover generation" where they were being taught and brought into a brand-new understanding and teaching about God. Because of the New Covenant, God's Presence no longer existing in the Temple which was soon to be completely destroyed but instead had now taken up residence in the hearts and lives of His newly formed Church—the Saints—the Believers in Jesus Christ as Messiah!

So, in essence at the time of the writing of these passages two things were happening:

- The physical Old Covenant Temple was still standing and sacrifices were still being offered up to God.
- The new idea of the Church was being taught and demonstrated, revealing that God had changed residences—He now had a new address and those sacrifices were no longer needed as they would soon come to a complete and permanent end with the destruction of the Temple. Which occurred circa AD70.

The next section of this chapter will be taken from a set of teachings by Pastor David B. Curtis of the Berean Bible Church at 1000 Chattanooga Street, Chesapeake, VA 23322, USA. You can visit them on the World Wide Web at the following address: http://www.bereanbiblechurch.org/studies/eschatology.php

Proverbs 2:1-5

My son, if you receive my words, And treasure my commands within you, So that you incline your ear to wisdom, And apply your heart to understanding; Yes, if you cry out for discernment, And lift up your voice for understanding, If you seek her as silver, And search for her as for hidden treasures; Then you will understand the fear of the LORD, *And find the knowledge of God.*

"Understanding the Bible." I'm sure that you are aware that is not a simple thing to do. All you have to do is look around at all the different churches with all their different beliefs, which they say come from the Bible, and it is easy to see that understanding the Bible is not that easy.

When the 12 early Disciples [later Apostles] of Jesus Christ heard Him speak about future events they had an idea in mind about what He meant. This is called "audience relevance." Simply stated, audience relevance is what the message meant to its original hearers.

The events of the New Testament are close to 2,000 years old. The audience relevance of what was said or seen is very important in understanding the Bible. However, those thoughts, beliefs and concepts that the original hearers had, have been to a large extent, either lost or completely distorted over the years.

When we read and study the Bible, we consciously or unconsciously, read into it what we believe to be true. Those preconceived ideas can come from what we have been taught or what some authority figure, i.e. Pastor, Teacher or another Author has spoken. We can call this "baggage" because it is often something we carry around that slows us down and dictates how we look at things.

There are good and godly men who disagree about every doctrine the Bible teaches. Some read the Bible and end up Armenians, and others read the same Bible and are Calvinists. Some study Scripture and are Charismatic, others study the same Scripture and are not Charismatic. When it comes to the subject of Eschatology, the *"end times"*, we have Dispensationalists, some of whom are Pre-trib, Mid-trib, or Post trib. We also have Pre-millennialists, Post-millennialists and Amillennialists. Then we have Partial-Preterist, Full-Preterist and Hyper-Preterist. Wow! They all read the same Bible, and yet they see things so differently. This should tell us that understanding the Bible is not a simple task.

If we are going to understand the Bible, we must have some understanding of Hermeneutics. Hermeneutics is the science of Biblical interpretation. The purpose of Hermeneutics is to establish guidelines and rules for interpreting the Bible. Any written document is subject to misinterpretation, and thus we have developed rules to safeguard us from such misunderstanding.

[1]At the beginning of the Middle Ages, Augustine of Hippo (354-430) expressed New Testament priority with the phrase, "The New is in the Old concealed; the Old is in the New revealed." Augustine meant that the Old Testament contains shadowy types and figures that are only clearly revealed in the New Testament. In other words, the New Testament explains the Old Testament. The Protestant Reformers and Puritans also looked to the New Testament to govern their interpretation of the Old.

The interpretive principle of New Testament priority is derived from an examination of the Scriptures themselves. As we read the Bible, we

---

[1] Author's comment and not from quoted text.

notice that earlier texts never explicitly interpret later texts. Earlier texts provide the interpretive context for later texts, but earlier texts never cite later texts and explain them directly. Rather, what we find is that later texts make explicit reference to earlier texts and provide explanations of them. Moreover, the later portion of any book always makes clear the earlier portion.

The hermeneutical principle of New Testament priority simply recognizes these facts. Following the Bible's own example, interpreters should allow later revelation in Bible to explain earlier revelation, rather than insisting on their own uninspired interpretations of earlier revelation without reference to the authoritative explanations of later revelation.[2]

God has spoken, and what He has said is recorded in Scripture. The basic need of Hermeneutics is to ascertain what God meant by what He said. For example: Matthew 5:39-42

> *But I tell you not to resist an evil person. But whoever slaps you on your right cheek, turn the other to him also. If anyone wants to sue you and take away your tunic, let him have your cloak also. And whoever compels you to go one mile, go with him two. Give to him who asks you, and from him who wants to borrow from you do not turn away.*

Is this to be taken literally? This is an important question, is it not? So, what do you think, are these commands to be taken literally? If you say, "Yes, these are to be taken literally," then I'm going to ask you for your car keys. Jesus said, *"Give to Him who asks you."* So, I'm asking you to give me your car keys. If you take this literally, then you must give me your car keys. Do you see the problem here? If you give me the car keys, I can legally take your car even though you may not like anyone driving your car.

So, how do we know if these verses are to be taken literally or not? Good question, I'm glad you asked. We all know what Jesus said. The important question is, "What did He mean by what He said?" How do we determine that? We are to determine what the Bible means by the use of Hermeneutics.

---

[2] End of author's quote. Taken from https://founders.org/2016/05/26/hermeneutics-new-testament-priority

Now, we don't have time to go through all the principles of Hermeneutics, but I want to deal with two of them that I feel are not well understood and are critical to a proper understanding of Scripture.

The primary rule of Hermeneutics is called: "The Analogy of Faith"—this means that Scripture interprets Scripture. No part of Scripture can be interpreted in such a way as to render it in conflict with what is clearly taught elsewhere in Scripture. The analogy of faith is a safeguard that should help us from reading into the Scriptures something that is not there. If one Scripture seems to contradict another, then we must turn to what is easily understood and then continue digging until we have reconciled the apparent contradiction or difficult understanding. God is not the author of confusion, and I believe His word is adequately clear to show us the answers.

"The Westminster Confession of Faith" states, "The infallible rule of interpretation of Scripture, is the Scripture itself; and therefore, when there is a question about the true and full sense of any Scripture (which is not manifold, but one), it must be searched and known by other places that speak more clearly."

Under the principle of the analogy of faith I want to bring up an aspect of this point that I have come to believe is vital in understanding the Bible. It is this: The Bible is one book. It is my opinion that the designation of the Old Testament as being "old" is destructive. We think of something old as being outdated or not needed any longer. When I buy a new laptop with all the bells and whistles, I no longer want to use my "old" one but I might need some files on the desktop or hard drive. I will have to copy the files over to access them if I use my new laptop singularly. Hence, I can't discount the old one in favour of the new.

I think that most Christians have the idea that the Old Testament is neither needed nor useful for Believers. This is due in part to confusing the Old Covenant, which has been superseded by the New Covenant, to the Old Testament. We connect the Old Covenant and the Old Testament, and since the Old Covenant passed away, we believe so has the Old Testament. The Old Covenant is fulfilled, and we are under the New Covenant. But the First Testament is not "old."

Please understand this: Apart from understanding the First Testament, "you will never completely understand the Second Testament. The writers of the Second Testament all suppose that their readers understood the

First Testament. Look at Romans 1: "*Paul, a bond-servant of Christ Jesus, called as an apostle, set apart for the gospel of God, which He promised beforehand through His prophets in the holy Scriptures,*" (Romans 1:1-2 NASB)

What is Paul saying here? He is saying that the Gospel was promised in the First Testament. "*Through His prophets in the holy Scriptures*" is referring to the First Testament.

To understand the words of the Second Testament, we must understand the words of the First Testament. For example, the new Believer begins to read the Bible and starts in Matthew: "*The book of the genealogy of Jesus Christ, the son of David, the son of Abraham.*" (Matthew 1:1 NASB)

In the first verse of the so-called New Testament, we have to ask, "Who is David? Who is Abraham? "Where do we get the answers to those questions? We have to go back to the First Testament. The New Testament is a continuance and completion of the first Testament or Old Testament.

Speaking of Mary, Matthew writes—"*And she will bear a Son; and you shall call His name Jesus, for it is He who will save His people from their sins.*" (Matthew 1:21 NASB)

Who are "*His people*?" The First Testament will answer that with the tribe of Israel! Matthew then tells us that this was in fulfillment of prophecy from the First Testament: "*Now all this took place that what was spoken by the Lord through the prophet might be fulfilled, saying,*" (Matthew 1:22 NASB) Then He quotes from Isaiah:

BEHOLD, THE VIRGIN SHALL BE WITH CHILD, AND SHALL BEAR A SON, AND THEY SHALL CALL HIS NAME IMMANUEL," *which when translated, means,* "*GOD WITH US.*" (Matthew 1:23 NASB)

So, the Virgin Mary giving birth to Jesus was foretold in the First Testament.

Then in chapter two it is said of Herod: "*And gathering together all the chief priests and scribes of the people, he began to inquire of them where the Christ was to be born. And they said to him, "In Bethlehem of Judea, for so it has been written by the prophet,*" (Matthew 2:4-5 NASB)

Then He quotes again from the First Testament, this time from Micah: "*'AND YOU, BETHLEHEM, LAND OF JUDAH, ARE BY NO MEANS LEAST AMONG THE LEADERS OF JUDAH; FOR OUT OF YOU SHALL COME FORTH A RULER, WHO WILL SHEPHERD MY PEOPLE ISRAEL.'*" (Matthew 2:6 NASB)

So, from these few examples of inter-twining Scripture, we become acquainted with many facts about Jesus from the First Testament.

God is the ultimate author of the Bible, and nothing came forth from a human hand with regards to prophecy and this important truth has implications for how we understand it.

To understand the words of the Second Testament, we must understand the words of the First Testament. Let me try to demonstrate this to you. When the new believer who is reading Matthew comes to chapter 24 and reads: "*But immediately after the tribulation of those days THE SUN WILL BE DARKENED, AND THE MOON WILL NOT GIVE ITS LIGHT, AND THE STARS WILL FALL from the sky, and the powers of the heavens will be shaken,*" (Matthew 24:29 NASB)

How does he/she understand "sun, moon, and stars?" He/she would most likely think in a literal way of the heavenly bodies. But if he/she were familiar with the "First Testament," he/she would have a different idea. So let's go to the First Testament and see how sun, moon, and stars are used other than in a literal way. Where do we start? How about Genesis?

> *Now he had still another dream, and related it to his brothers, and said, "Lo, I have had still another dream; and behold, the sun and the moon and eleven stars were bowing down to me."* (Genesis 37:9 NASB)

Is Joseph's dream about the literal sun and moon and stars bowing to him? How would the sun bow down? This may confuse us, but Joseph's father knew exactly what he was saying: "*And he related it to his father and to his brothers; and his father rebuked him and said to him, "What is this dream that you have had? Shall I and your mother and your brothers actually come to bow ourselves down before you to the ground?*" (Genesis 37:10 NASB)

Jacob, Joseph's father, interprets this dream as referring to himself, his wife, and their sons, who were the heads of the twelve tribes identified as the sun, moon, and stars, respectively. They represented the foundation of the whole Jewish nation. When Jesus, therefore, spoke of the sun being darkened, the moon not giving its light, and the stars falling from heaven, He was not referring to the end of the solar system, but of the complete dissolution of the Jewish state.

This apocalyptic language is common among the Hebrew Prophets. This idea is seen clearly as we look at passages where mention is made of the destruction of a state and government using language which seems to set forth the end of the world:

The oracle concerning Babylon which Isaiah the son of Amos saw— (Isaiah 13:1 NASB)

In this chapter God is talking about the judgement that is to fall upon Babylon. The word "oracle" is the Hebrew word massa, which means: "an utterance, chiefly a doom." This introduction sets the stage for the subject matter in this chapter. And if we forget this, our interpretations of Isaiah 13 can go just about anywhere our imagination wants to go. This is not an oracle against the universe or world, but against the nation of Babylon.

Wail, for the day of the LORD is near! It will come as destruction from the Almighty. (Isaiah 13:6 NASB)

Behold, the day of the LORD is coming, Cruel, with fury and burning anger, To make the land a desolation; And He will exterminate its sinners from it. For the stars of heaven and their constellations Will not flash forth their light; The sun will be dark when it rises, And the moon will not shed its light. Thus I will punish the world for its evil, And the wicked for their iniquity; I will also put an end to the arrogance of the proud, And abase the haughtiness of the ruthless. I will make mortal man scarcer than pure gold, And mankind than the gold of Ophir. Therefore I shall make the heavens tremble, And the earth will be shaken from its place At the fury of the LORD of hosts In the day of His burning anger. (Isaiah 13:9-13 NASB)

Now remember, he is speaking about the destruction of Babylon, but is sounds like worldwide destruction. The terminology of a context cannot be expanded beyond the scope of the subject under discussion. The spectrum of language surely cannot go outside the land of Babylon. If you were a Babylonian, and Babylon was destroyed, would it seem like the world was destroyed? Yes! Your world would be destroyed.

Behold, I am going to stir up the Medes against them, Who will not value silver or take pleasure in gold, (Isaiah 13:17 NASB)

This is a historical event that took place in 539 B.C. When the Medes destroyed Babylon, the Babylonian world came to an end. This destruction is said, in verse 6, to be from the Almighty, and the Medes constitute the means that God uses to accomplish this task. This is apocalyptic language. This is the way the Bible discusses the fall of a nation. This is obviously figurative language. God did not intend for us to take this literally. If we take this literally, the world ended in 539 B.C.

So, when Matthew talks about the "sun, moon, and stars" falling from the sky, he is not talking about the end of planet earth, he is talking about the end of Israel the Old Covenant. This understanding is critical! But if we do not understand the language of the first three quarters of the Bible, we will never understand the last quarter of the New Testament.

The Bible was written in a time, far distant from ours, and in cultures quite strange to us. So, as we try to discover the author's meaning, we must learn to read his writing as one of his contemporaries would. To do this we must understand the First Testament as they did. For example, when you read: "*BEHOLD, HE IS COMING WITH THE CLOUDS, and every eye will see Him, even those who pierced Him; and all the tribes of the earth will mourn over Him. Even so. Amen.*" (Revelation 1:7 NASB)

We have all kinds of strange ideas as to what this means, but if we are familiar with the First Testament, we know that the Lord is often depicted as riding a cloud (Psalms 18:7-15, Psalms 68:4; 104:3; Nahum 1:3). As we place the Biblical image in the light of the ancient Near East, we realize that God's cloud is a chariot that He rides bringing judgment. So, when the Second Testament talks about Jesus riding a cloud, we understand that this is not a white, fluffy cloud, but a storm cloud that He rides into judgment. The more we understand the first Testament, the better we will understand the language of the Second Testament.

Jesus said that the First Testament spoke of Him: "*You search the Scriptures, because you think that in them you have eternal life; and it is these that bear witness of Me;*" (John 5:39 NASB)

[Apostle] Paul, when standing before King Agrippa said this: "*And so, having obtained help from God, I stand to this day testifying both to small and great, stating nothing but what the Prophets and Moses said was going to take place*" (Acts 26:22 NASB)

According to this verse, what was the content of *[Apostle]* Paul's preaching? It was the First Testament! Does this help you understand the importance of the First Testament?

Now let me share with you another rule of Hermeneutics that will greatly help us in our study of Acts. Remember that **Biblical hermeneutics** is the study of the principles of interpretation concerning the books of the Bible.

As stated earlier in this book, the second rule of Hermeneutics is audience relevance. This means that whatever a passage meant, or whatever words spoken in Scripture meant, it had direct application to the original intended audience.

To demonstrate that many do not understand this principle, notice what one pastor wrote: "You know the Bible is timeless. Let's look at these Scriptures as though *[Apostle]* Paul had just sent an email to the local assembly of the Church of God." It sounds cool to think of it in this way, but holding this view will keep you from understanding the Bible.

I think that most Christians view the Bible this way—like it just arrived in the mail for you. But we must understand that if we disengage the original audience from the Scriptures, then we can make any passage mean whatever we want, or apply them in whatever mode we want, even to the point of justifying sinful behaviours. Whenever we read the Scriptures, we must ask ourselves, "Who is this person talking or writing directly to?" We must remember that the Bible is a collection of personal letters and history books written by real people, to real people, in real time, and with real time contexts.

For instance, in the book of Philippians the *[Apostle]* Paul wrote the following:

> *But I hope in the Lord Jesus to send Timothy to you shortly, so that I also may be encouraged when I learn of your condition. (Philippians 2:19 NASB)*

Does this verse teach us that we are supposed to be still waiting on Timothy today so that he can take word back to *[Apostle]* Paul on how we're doing? No, definitely not! Why not? Because we correctly understand audience relevance, and that this was a personal letter from *[Apostle]* Paul to a real church in Philippi in A.D. 62 about an event (sending *[Apostle]* Timothy) that was imminent to them, not to us. We correctly understand the time and place context. The Philippians are the intended audience of this book. *[Apostle]* Timothy would be a decayed cadaver if we were waiting for him to arrive in our present day.

All time statements in the Bible must be viewed through this same lens of audience relevance. The books of the Bible are not mystical letters written nebulously to Christians throughout eternity whereby all "time" statements are free to be extracted and applied to whatever generation we wish. No, each book was directed to a specific audience, and again, Scripture is more than adequate to show us who that audience was.

As stated earlier, in keeping with the subject of audience relevance, this may perhaps shock many people, but there is not one book in the Bible that was written TO any specific person living today. Every single book in the Bible was written FOR us who are alive on planet earth today for application and understanding, but none of them were written TO us. Every book in the Bible is a personal letter, a history book, or writing by a Prophet to particular people at a particular time and for a particular reason.

Yes, we do glean truth and understanding from these books today, but that is far different than saying that these books were written TO us. To put it another way, we are reading other people's mail. Whenever someone today says, "Here's what this Scripture means to me", we should be the first to say, "It doesn't matter what it means to you. It only matters what it meant to the original audience." That is where we find out what the Bible truly means. Only after we do that can we then apply it to ourselves.

Believer, I've got some bad news for you, which is my third point in understanding the Bible: It takes a lot of time and hard work to understand the Bible. Yet many Christians who are lazy and very casual in their approach to Bible study say they want to understand it:

The soul of the sluggard craves and gets nothing, But the soul of the diligent is made fat. (Proverbs 13:4 NASB)

Let me see if I can illustrate this for you. Who do you think was the highest paid professional athlete in 2006? It was Tiger Woods. In 2006 Woods earned an estimated $100 million from winnings and endorsements. Golf Digest predicted that Woods would have become the world's first billionaire athlete in 2010. Woods is the most successful golfer of all time.

When did Tiger Woods start working on fine-tuning his golf game? Did he start in early adulthood and work on it one hour a week? Isn't that what most Christians do with Bible study? And tragically, that one hour a week for most Christians is not much of a learning time; it's more of a story time. Tiger began at two years old and worked hour after hour perfecting his craft. There is no doubt that he is an extremely gifted man, but he is what he is because of a lot of hard work.

In our studies we have seen that the Jews from early childhood would work on memorizing the Scriptures. By the time a boy was 12, he had the Torah memorized. That is a lot of work. So why do we think we can listen to one message on the Bible once a week and read it maybe once or twice a week and come to understand it? Why are we so arrogant and lazy that we spend no time in the book and yet get frustrated and even angry when we can't understand it?

My son, if you will receive my sayings, And treasure my commandments within you, Make your ear attentive to wisdom, Incline your heart to understanding; For if you cry for discernment, Lift your voice for understanding; If you seek her as silver, And search for her as for hidden treasures; Then you will discern the fear of the LORD, And discover the knowledge of God. (Proverbs 2:1-5 NASB)

Do you cry out to God for Biblical understanding? Do you search the Scriptures with the same diligence that drives you to earn money? Understanding the Bible takes a huge TIME commitment. Is God worthy of your time?

One of the greatest problems in the Church today is ignorance. There are some people who have been Christians for ten or twenty years, but know next to nothing about the Bible. God doesn't tolerate ignorance.

The Nineteenth century English preacher, Charles H. Spurgeon, was right when he said: "We're to eat into the very heart of the Bible until at last we come to talk in Scriptural language and our spirits are flavoured with the words of the Lord, so that the very essence of the Bible flows from us!"

What are you doing right now to assure that you develop a thorough knowledge of God's Word? The range of possibilities is wide and endless: You can commit yourself to a daily Bible-reading schedule, take notes during Bible study meetings, read good Christian books, enter into discipleship with a mature Christian, take classes or a correspondence course with a Christian college, or listen to good Christian teachers on television or radio. Make sure you are receiving nourishment daily from God's Word using one or more of those avenues for learning. The best way to make sure you make progress is to meet regularly with a good Christian friend to share with each other what you're learning so that you may *"grow in grace, and in the knowledge of our Lord and Saviour, Jesus Christ"* (2 Peter 3:18).

You might ask, "Why exert so much effort to Bible study?" I'll tell you why because Scripture is the self-revelation of God. In it the mind and heart of God is laid bare on many matters. With knowledge of Scripture, we learn who God is and what He values. In the Bible God reveals Himself for who He is!

If we are going to understand the Bible, we need to understand the rules of Hermeneutics and apply them to our study. Scripture interprets Scripture, and along with this we must realize that the Bible is ONE book. We must also apply audience relevance. And we must be willing to devote much time and energy to the Bible. Again, I ask you, "Is God worthy of your time? Does your commitment to Scripture demonstrate that He is worthy of your time?"

DEATH AND RESURRECTION
I was raised in Church believing that Enoch and Elijah were taken directly to Heaven without dying, something that most Believers believe. Maybe you have been taught that also. Personally, I have never known anyone that questioned this fact, but is that really what the Bible teaches? It seems like such an insignificant thing. Why would what happen to Enoch and Elijah make any difference to us in our lifetime? God can do what He wants in whatever way He wants, can't He? Let's find out if this causes any problems with understanding the Bible and Yahweh Himself.

And as it is appointed unto men once to die, but after this the judgment: (Hebrews 9:27 KJV)

The Young's Literal Translation makes the statement even stronger:

and as it is laid up to men once to die, and after this--judgment, (Hebrews 9:27 YLT)

And Enoch walked with God: and he was not; for God took him. (Genesis 5:24)

By faith Enoch was translated that he should not see death; and was not found, because God had translated him: for before his translation he had this testimony, that he pleased God. (Hebrews 11:5)

These **all died in faith***, not having received the promises, but having seen them afar off, and were persuaded of them, and embraced them, and confessed that they were strangers and pilgrims on the earth.* (Emphasis Author's) (Hebrews 11:13)

A HERITAGE OF DEATH

Thanks to Adam we all can expect to die. Romans 5:12, "*Wherefore, as by one man sin entered into the world, and death by sin; and so death passed upon all men, for that all have sinned:*" In fact, according to Hebrews 9:27 we cannot escape it. Who does "all" include in Romans 5:12? Does it include you and me? How about every man that has ever lived from Adam on? It is simple to see that "all" means everyone that has ever lived, including Christ. (Some have dared to say that "all" does not mean "all" but that is a rabbit trail we don't want to go down for this study. Some men will always try to deny simple truth.)

    The Bible describes two deaths. One is the physical death we all must go through. The second is a death, which we do not have to endure. That is the death of eternal separation from Yahweh also known as the second death in Revelation 2:11, "*He that hath an ear, let him hear what the Spirit saith unto the churches; He that overcometh shall not be hurt of the second death.*" KJV

THE ANSWER—DEATH, BURIAL, RESURRECTION

According to Hebrews 9:27, every person must experience a physical death but because of the sacrifice that Christ paid by the shedding of his blood and death we can escape the second death. Victory over death through resurrection! That is the manifestation of following and trusting in the blood of our Saviour. That is the example of Christ, which we all must follow. Only because of Christ's defeating death, by being faithful to Yahweh, can we also experience and enjoy that victory also.

Death, burial, resurrection. That is the Gospel, plain and simple. Hebrews 9:27 makes it plain that every person must meet death. Death to the Believer, however, is really only a new beginning. The beginning of eternal life, through resurrection, in a new, sinless body.

That concept however presents a problem according to much teaching today. It is commonly taught that Enoch and Elijah did not die. It is further taught in many religious circles, that many will not experience death if they are alive when the "*rapture*" occurs.

TRADITIONAL TEACHING CREATES A PROBLEM

That concept contradicts Scripture and the example Christ set before us. So how do we reason this problem out? Many have said that God can do what He wants and that is true in concept. However, if Yahweh determines to make His Word conditional or creates special exemptions, He would be bound by His nature to make that plainly known. Does God want to be known as having no rhyme or reason for His actions? No, He wants to be known as consistent, solid, and never wavering. When we trust God we can be sure He will provide a straight and steady course for us to follow. He will not suddenly change direction on us, leaving us confused and questioning our safety.

To consider that the Almighty Everlasting God would provide an escape from physical death for many without providing that for His own son does not make sense. If there were another way to victory other than through death, burial and resurrection, He would have surely provided that option to His Son.

HIDING IN PLAIN SIGHT

As is so often the case with Bible matters, the answer is hiding in plain sight. Regarding Enoch, Hebrews 11:5 appears to say that Enoch never died. Reading this verse along with Genesis 5:24 would seem to confirm that idea. However, it contradicts the mandate of Hebrews 9:27 and Romans 5:12. The truth about Enoch is found in Hebrews 11:13, *"These all died..."* Enoch died just as did all of the other Old Covenant Believers listed in Hebrews chapter 11. There it is in black-and-white. Have you ever seen that before? So many gems are hiding in plain sight.

So, how do we reason out these Scriptures? Notice that *"God took him"* but it does not say "where" He took him. If indeed Yahweh took him to Heaven another Scripture would have been violated when Christ said, *"And no man hath ascended up to heaven, but he that came down from heaven, even the Son of man which is in heaven."* (John 3:13)

The same can be said of Elijah. So, what happened to Enoch? Evidently God transported him to another place. From what is said in Hebrews 11:5, his life must have been in imminent danger and God spared him and transported him to a place of safety.

James 4:4 *"Ye adulterers and adulteresses, know ye not that the friendship of the world is enmity with God? Whosoever therefore will be a friend of the world is the enemy of God."* Conversely, it could be said, if a man is the friend of God, as Enoch was, he will be the enemy of the world. Is it possible that there were people that would have liked to see Enoch dead? It seems a possibility to me but the writer of Hebrews does not expound upon the reason.

MORE BIBLE EXPLANATION

By understanding the story of Elijah, we learn even more about these occurrences. Dr. Ron McRay has expertly covered this subject in greater detail in his book, "Is It Appointed Unto Man Once To Die?" He shows from the Bible how the idea of being supernaturally transported (think Star Trek) was a reality several times in the Bible. It is well worth reading to discover how these apparent exceptions were not exceptions at all. Yahweh is faithful to His Word! [End of teaching by Pastor David B. Curtis]

Let us be careful not to interject into God's Word what our imaginations conjure up. The Bible cannot contradict itself and God cannot violate His Word. He is not trying to trick us or cause us to be confused. He is not a mystical being that goes about doing things that cannot be explained. Today we are caught up into believing seemingly mystical and magical events and allowing those emotions to carry over into our reading and understanding of the Bible. Trust God to act and perform in accordance with His Word. You will be blessed by that understanding as you study the Bible further.

CHAPTER TWO
AN IMPORTANT QUESTION

IF YOU STATE THAT SCRIPTURE WAS WRITTEN TO A 1ST CENTURY AUDIENCE AND HAS been fulfilled largely in that 1st Century, how do you explain **the "final" Resurrection of the dead *AFTER* Christ's resurrection and ascension?** This question was posed during a Q and A session at our local assembly, which then gave birth to this book you are presently reading. My response was this: **One question before we proceed: what happens to the Saints who die today?** The following was my answer and as you read, see if you would agree with me.

Before answering the question let me first of all say this: nowhere does the Bible teach about a "final" resurrection. That is something that has been read into the Bible, gained from man's reasoning of Scripture and him placing his own take on the Word of God. Search as much as you want you will not find the words "final resurrection" anywhere in the Bible. It is a doctrinal belief shared by many denominations and has been accepted as a universal truth due to this reasoning and speculation.

Here is what the Scripture say:

We are confident, yes, well pleased rather to be absent from the body and to be present with the Lord. (2 Corinthians 5:8)

Also, I submitted the idea that while I believe that the New Testament was written to a 1st Century people and was fulfilled with that 1st Century audience, and that I also believe that the Scriptures have that ability to be relevant back then and relevant to us today and will continue to be relevant tomorrow and in the millennia to come!

The member [the Saint] went on to make the following comments and posed another question, so bear with me a little as we navigate the twists and turns of our journey. The Saint cited the following Scripture: 1 Corinthians 15:51-54

> *Listen, I tell you a mystery: We will not all sleep, but we will all be changed—in a flash, in the twinkling of an eye, at <u>the last trumpet</u>. For <u>the trumpet will sound</u>, the dead will be raised imperishable, and we will be changed. For the perishable must clothe itself with the imperishable, and the mortal with immortality. When the perishable has been clothed with the imperishable, and the mortal with immortality, then the saying that is written will come true: "Death has been swallowed up in victory." (Emphasis Author's) NIV*

My response was first in the form of a question: what last trumpet is the *[Apostle]* Paul referring to here? **Most folks believe it is talking about the last trumpet of time. I can tell you that this is not what is being referred to here. This will be discussed later in this book!**

The Saint continued: The context of this Scripture is in *[Apostle]* Paul's chapter about the reality of the *resurrection*. <u>The whole purpose of the chapter was to persuade the Believers that resurrection is real</u>. So *[Apostle]* Paul is NOT talking metaphorically as that would be an unscriptural interpretation.

My response: Of course *[Apostle]* Paul was indeed speaking of a real resurrection. After all he was speaking to a group of newly converted Saints who were steeped in the understanding of the Old Covenant, and as such he was bringing them up to "code" ... In essence he was actually being used by God to write and establish the New Testament, while the Old was still operating... Do you understand this? Are you seeing this?

Just to give some context to the Scriptures: We have the situation here where this Old Covenant Temple, which was ordained and mandated by God to be built, and was the headquarters for law and order in the earth. Everything sprung from that place. Then at the appointed time this huge miracle took place—Jesus was born of a Virgin and stepped into the public life of the Jews, to not only fulfill the Old Testament Law, but to also introduce brand new laws and a new way of living.

Of course, many of them struggled with Him and with what He brought, as they saw it conflicting with what they understood God had ordained for them to walk and function in.

So, now after His [Jesus'] death, burial and resurrection the *[Apostle]* Paul is teaching concerning this NEW WAY. That this NEW WAY was as a result of the finished work of Calvary and what Jesus had accomplished—at death, that they no longer had to wait to be in the Presence of the Lord! His teaching included that they had just ONE GENERATION to understand that once the Temple was destroyed God had made His decision clear and plain for all to know that He made the switch from wood and stone in the form of the Temple to living in the HEARTS of those who now accepted Jesus Christ as their Saviour and as their Lord. That this was now His new HEADQUARTERS! Their lives! The Church known as the Body of Believers!

So once we got to circa AD70 when the destruction of the Temple occurred, that was it. No longer would men have to go and sleep in the grave or wherever they went before Jesus came and paid the price and purchased our Salvation. No, they now went straight to be with the Lord at death!

So in essence he was saying to them, "hey please understand that when a person dies that person no longer goes to sleep [as was the custom under the Old system, before Christ came and died and rose again] but that person is changed in the twinkling of an eye and is transported into the Presence of the Lord." That it was immediate and there was no need to wait.

Here's another thing we have to take into consideration: And again *[Apostle]* Paul is speaking to 1st Century Believers while the Old Covenant Temple was still standing. At a time when most of them believed that when a person died they were going to sleep and wait for the resurrection!

Behold, I tell you a mystery: We shall not all sleep, but we shall all be changed... 1 Corinthians 15:51

Before this statement, he shared this explanation, which speaks of such a change.

And what you sow, you do not sow that body that shall be, but mere grain—perhaps wheat or some other grain: (1 Corinthians 15:37)

The seed of a plant that goes into the ground changes into another form. It is not left there as a seed. It germinates into the stalk of the plant.

For example: When I dig up a plant, I do not see a seed that did not change, but rather I see roots, soil and a stalk which are a result of the "**changed**" seed. The seed has been transformed into the stalk and plant!

The Saint then quoted the following passage of Scripture followed by some comments:

Brothers and sisters, we do not want you to be uninformed about those who sleep in death, so that you do not grieve like the rest of mankind, who have no hope. For we believe that Jesus died and rose again, *and so we believe that God will bring with Jesus those who have fallen asleep in him. According to the Lord's word, we tell you that we who are still alive, who are left until the coming of the Lord, will certainly not precede those who have fallen asleep.* **For the Lord himself will come down from heaven, with a loud command, with the voice of the archangel and with the trumpet call of God, and the dead in Christ will rise first**. NIV [Emphasis Author's] 1 Thessalonians 4:13-16

Verses 16-17 seems to also refer to a *resurrection*, since, as a pre-cursor, in verse 14, *[Apostle]* Paul refers to the death and resurrection of Jesus Christ. As well, from verse 13, it seems that the purpose of the verses that follow seeks to encourage those who have lost loved ones. It is an assurance that those who have died will *rise* to be with Christ as Christ himself rose from the dead, and that we also will rise to be with Christ. <u>A figurative interpretation seems a stretch without a clear Scriptural basis</u>.

My response: Of course, that is correct but once again we must look at the context of that passage, as I have done here: 1 Thessalonians 4:13-18

Brothers and sisters, [<u>whom was he speaking to here? Yes 1st Century Believers</u>] we do not want you to be uninformed about those who sleep in death, so that you do not grieve like the rest of mankind, who have no hope. For we believe that Jesus died and rose again, and so we believe that God will bring with Jesus those who have fallen asleep in him *[<u>who are those that have fallen asleep in Him? Yes the Old Covenant Saints…</u>]. According to the Lord's word, we tell you that we who are still alive, who are left until the coming of the Lord, will certainly not precede those who have fallen asleep.* **For the Lord himself will come down from heaven, with a loud command, with the voice of the archangel and with the trumpet call of God, and the dead in Christ will rise first. After that, we [<u>who is the we he is referring to here? Those to whom he was speaking…</u>] who are still alive and are left will be caught up together with them in the clouds to meet the Lord in the air. And so we will be with the Lord forever. Therefore encourage one another [<u>who are these one another spoken of here? Yes of course the early Church Saints he was speaking to</u>] with these words**. NIV [Emphasis Author's]

The Saint then referenced the following passage: 2 Timothy 2:17-18

Their teaching will spread like gangrene. Among them are Hymenaeus and Philetus, who have departed from the truth. They say that the resurrection has already taken place, and they destroy the faith of some.

My response: Again, *[Apostle]* Paul was speaking to 1st Century Believers and of course Hymenaeus and Philetus were wrong at that time to declare that the resurrection was past. At that time of the writing of Paul to Timothy the resurrection had not yet taken place because the Old Covenant Temple was still standing. So that instruction was correct, but to say that today almost 2,000 years removed from that time is incorrect and a wrong application or interpretation of Scripture. More on this later!

The Saint's response: *[Apostle]* Paul is talking about a resurrection event (not several) *still* to take place. *So what resurrection is Paul talking about in all of these above Scriptures? When is this resurrection supposed to have happened (if indeed it has already happened)?*

My response is in the following teaching from several other authors and teachers that I agree with and thought it best to just quote them here. And please understand that this book is not a work that was done for profit. No! It was done to give the Saints a valuable teaching about this most important subject of "death and the resurrection" in my estimation. In doing so I also felt that it would be of benefit to the wider Body, the Church—so here goes!

The next chapter will be taken from a set of teachings from Pastor David B. Curtis of the Berean Bible Church at 1000 Chattanooga Street, Chesapeake, VA 23322, USA. For more of his teachings you can visit them on the World Wide Web at the following address: http://www.bereanbiblechurch.org/studies/eschatology.php

CHAPTER THREE
THE SECOND COMING AND ETERNAL LIFE OR WHERE ARE THE DEAD?

who shall not receive a hundredfold now in this time—houses and brothers and sisters and mothers and children and lands, with persecutions—and in the age to come, eternal life. (Mark 10:30)

WHEN A CHRISTIAN DIES, WHERE DOES HE [SHE] GO? NOW, YOU MIGHT THINK that that is a stupid question because everyone knows that Christians go to Heaven. Right? Since when? When did Christians start going to Heaven when they died?

Several weeks ago, my eleven-year-old daughter, Lindsey, asked her Christian schoolteacher this question, "If you were to die right now where would you go?" The teacher responded, "To Heaven." Lindsey then asked her, "How could you go to Heaven if Jesus has not returned yet?" Her teacher said, "Well, different people believe different things." Lindsey said, "They sure do!"

I think that all Christians believe that when a Believer dies, they go to Heaven. But why? If you pinned them down and asked for some Scriptural proof, they might share two verses with you.

2 Corinthians 5:8

We are confident, yes, well pleased rather to be absent from the body and to be present with the Lord.

Philippians 1:23

For I am hard pressed between the two, having a desire to depart and be with Christ, which is far better.

Most Christians would say, "[*Apostle*] Paul is teaching here that to be 'absent from the body' or 'to depart' (physical death) is to be with Christ in Heaven." I would agree with that but only because I believe that the "Second Coming" of Christ has already happened. Prior to the "Second Coming" of Christ, as Lindsey pointed out to her teacher, Believers didn't go to Heaven—they went to Hades to await the resurrection from the dead. So, if the Lord has not yet returned, then Believers do not go to Heaven at death. **The Bible teaches that apart from the resurrection, nobody goes to Heaven.** Let's see if we can prove this biblically.

As Christians, we believe that the Scripture is the self-revelation of God. In it the mind and heart of God is laid bare on many matters. With knowledge of Scripture we learn who God is and what He values. In the Bible, God reveals Himself. For this reason the study of the Bible should be a serious pursuit of every one of us.

In order to interpret the Bible correctly, we must have some understanding of Hermeneutics. **Hermeneutics** is the science of biblical interpretation.

Luke 24:27

And beginning at Moses and all the Prophets, He expounded to them in all the Scriptures the things concerning Himself.

The word "expounded" is the Greek word *diermeneuo,* which means: "to explain thoroughly, expound, interpret."

The purpose of hermeneutics is to establish guidelines and rules for interpreting the Bible. Any written document is subject to misinterpretation and thus we have developed rules to safeguard us from such misunderstanding.

God has spoken and what He has said is recorded in Scripture. The basic need of hermeneutics is to ascertain what **GOD MEANT BY WHAT HE SAID.**

As we read the Bible, we must keep in mind the hermeneutical principle of **"audience relevance"** which, seeks to discover what the **original** audience understood a passage to mean. The concern of the evangelical interpreter is to understand the grammar of a passage in light of the historical circumstances and context of the original audience.

In this writing we want to look at several areas of Scripture that we must understand in order to correctly understand when the dead were raised. The first thing we want to look at is that all through the New Testament we see **two ages** in contrast: "This age," and the "age to come."

Matthew 12:32

*Anyone who speaks a word against the Son of Man, it will be forgiven him; but whoever speaks against the Holy Spirit, it will not be forgiven him, either **in this age or in the age to come**.* (Emphasis Author's)

The word "come" at the end of the verse is the Greek word *mello*, which means: "about to be." We could translate this: "the age about to come." About to come for who? For the original audience, which were those in the First Century.

Ephesians 1:21

*far above all principality and power and might and dominion, and every name that is named, **not only in this age but also in that which is to come**.* (Emphasis Author's)

Here again, we see the reference to the two ages. So, the New Testament speaks of two ages, "this age," and "the age to come." The understanding of these two ages and when they changed is fundamental to interpreting the Bible and understanding when the dead went to Heaven.

The New Testament writers lived in the age that they called "this age." To the New Testament writers, "the age to come" was future, but it was very near because "this age" was about to end.

1 Corinthians 2:6-8

*However, we speak wisdom among those who are mature, yet **not the wisdom of this age, nor of the rulers of this age**, who are* *coming to nothing. But we speak the wisdom of God in a mystery, the hidden wisdom which God ordained before the ages for our glory, [8] which **none of the rulers of this age knew**; for had they known, they would not have crucified the Lord of glory.* (Emphasis Author's)

The wisdom and rulers of "this age" were coming to nothing because the age was passing away. He is speaking of the Jewish leaders and the Old Covenant system. The rulers of "this age" crucified the Lord. These rulers would shortly have no realm in which to rule because "this age" was about to end. Think about this, if the Jewish age ended at the cross, as so many claims, why were they still ruling the age?

1 Corinthians 10:11

*Now all these things happened to them as examples, and they were written for our admonition, upon whom **the ends of the ages have come**.* (Emphasis Author's)

[*Apostle*] Paul said very plainly that the end of the ages was coming upon them, the First Century Saints. "This age," along with its wisdom and rulers, was about to end.

1 Peter 1:20

*He indeed was foreordained before the foundation of the world, but was **manifest in these last times** for you.* (Emphasis Author's)

Jesus came during the "last days" of the "this age" that was the Old Covenant age, the Jewish age. That age came to an end with the destruction of the Temple [*circa*] AD 70. So, the New Testament writers lived in what the Bible calls "this age."

"This age" of the Bible is the age of the Old Covenant that was about to pass away in the First Century. It should be clear to you that "this age" is not the Christian age in which we live. In the First Century, the age of the Old Covenant was fading away and would end completely when the Temple was destroyed [*circa*] AD 70.

Hebrews 8:13

In that He says, "A new covenant," He has made the first obsolete. Now what is becoming obsolete and growing old is ready to vanish away.

The book of Hebrews was written at around 65-69 AD. At this time, the Old Covenant was still in effect but it was ready to pass away. It passed away in [*circa*] AD 70 in the destruction of Jerusalem. The "this age" of the Bible is now ancient history.

Alright, "this age" was about to end, and at the end of the Old Covenant age several things happened:

1. CHRIST RETURNED:
2 Timothy 4:1

I charge you therefore before God and the Lord Jesus Christ, who will (mello: about to come) judge the living and the dead at His appearing and His kingdom: (Parenthesis Author's)

Hebrews 10:37

For yet a little while, And He who is coming will come and will not tarry.

2. THE RESURRECTION OCCURRED:
John 11:24

Martha said to Him, "I know that he will rise again in the resurrection at the last day."

This was the "last day" of "this age," "the age to come" has no last days. So, the resurrection was to happen at the end of the Old Covenant age when the Lord returned.

3. THE JUDGMENT OCCURRED:
Matthew 13:40

Therefore as the tares are gathered and burned in the fire, so it will be at the end of this age.

Since the "present age" of the Bible ended in [*circa*] AD 70 with the destruction of the Temple and the coming of the Lord, we must be in "the age to come." And if we are in "the age to come," then the **resurrection has already happened**.

Notice what Jesus said the Believers would receive in the age to come.
Mark 10:29-30

*So, Jesus answered and said, "Assuredly, I say to you, there is no one who has left house or brothers or sisters or father or mother or wife or children or lands, for My sake and the gospel's, 30 who shall not receive a hundredfold now in this time; houses and brothers and sisters and mothers and children and lands, with persecutions; and in the **AGE TO COME, ETERNAL LIFE**."* (Emphasis Author's)

If eternal life was a condition of the "age to come," then does this mean that the New Testament Saints who lived in "this age" did not yet have eternal life? Or we could ask the question this way, "When did Believers receive eternal life?" To answer that question, we must know what "eternal life" is. Prior to Jesus' messianic work, no one went to Heaven.
John 3:13

No one has ascended to heaven but He who came down from heaven, that is, the Son of Man who is in heaven.

If prior to Jesus' messianic work, no one went to Heaven—where did people go when they died? They went to a holding place of the dead and waited for the atoning work of Christ and the resurrection from the dead. In the Old Testament, the Hebrew word for where they were prior to the resurrection is **Sheol**. In the New Testament, the Greek word is **Hades**. What this place amounted to was a waiting area for disembodied spirits.

God had promised to redeem His people from the grave.
Hosea 13:14

I will ransom them from the power of the grave; I will redeem them from death. O Death, I will be your plagues! O Grave, I will be your destruction! Pity is hidden from My eyes.

Psalms 49:15

But God will redeem my soul from the power of the grave, For He shall receive me. Selah

These verses express the hope that God will provide salvation beyond the grave, one of the few Old Testament references to life after death. This verse anticipates the clear New Testament teaching of life after death, and eternal life, and salvation from God.

Resurrection is: "resurrection from the dead." To understand death, we need to go back to the book of beginnings, Genesis. In the book of Genesis, we see what death is.

Genesis 2:15-17

Then the LORD God took the man and put him in the garden of Eden to tend and keep it. And the LORD God commanded the man, saying, "Of every tree of the garden you may freely eat; but of the tree of the knowledge of good and evil you shall not eat, for in the day that you eat of it you shall surely die."

God warned Adam, regarding the fruit from the tree of the knowledge of good and evil, *"The day that you eat of it, you shall surely die."* Adam disobeyed God and ate of the tree. Did Adam die that day? Not physically! Adam lived at least 800 years beyond the day he ate the fruit. But, God said he would die the day he ate, and we know that God cannot lie. Adam did not die physically that day, but he did die spiritually. He died spiritually the moment he disobeyed. Spiritual death is separation from God.

Isaiah 59:1-2

Behold, the Lord's hand is not shortened, That it cannot save; Nor His ear heavy, That it cannot hear. But your iniquities have separated you from your God; And your sins have hidden His face from you, So that He will not hear.

Because of his sin, man was separated from God. He was dead in trespasses and sins. The focus of God's plan of redemption is to restore through Jesus Christ what man had lost in Adam.
1 Corinthians 15:21

For since by man came death, (spiritual death) by Man also came the resurrection of the dead (eternal life). (Parenthesis Author's)

Because of Adam's sin, we are all born dead, separated from God. But through Jesus Christ came the resurrection from the dead. Jesus Christ came to redeem man from death, to resurrect man back into the presence of God. The Bible is God's book about His plan to restore the spiritual union of His creation. Resurrection is not about bringing physical bodies out of the graves, it is about restoring man into the presence of God. **To be taken out of Sheol and brought into the presence of the Lord is what the Bible calls the resurrection.** Daniel spoke of this in:
Daniel 12:2

And many of those who sleep in the dust of the ground will awake, these to everlasting life, but the others to disgrace and everlasting contempt. NASB

For Believers, the resurrection is to be given everlasting life. When was this resurrection to happen?
Daniel 12:13

But as for you, go your way to the end; then you will enter into rest and rise again for your allotted portion at THE END OF THE AGE. (Emphasis added) NASB

Jesus' answer to the Sadducees about the woman who had seven husbands indicates that the resurrection was to occur at the changing of the ages.

Luke 20:34-35

And Jesus answered and said to them, "The sons of <u>this age</u> (the Old Covenant age) marry and are given in marriage. But those who are counted worthy to attain <u>that age</u>, (the New Covenant age) and the resurrection from the dead, neither marry nor are given in marriage; (Emphasis and Parenthesis Author's)

The resurrection was not something that was available to them in "this age" (the Transition period, AD 30 to AD 70) but would be available to them in "that age" (the New Covenant age), implying that the resurrection would occur at the beginning of the New Covenant age.

So, the resurrection was to happen at the end of the Jewish age, the Old Covenant age. We know that this happened in [*circa*] AD 70 with the destruction of the Jewish temple. To be resurrected was to be given eternal life and to be in the presence of God.

We must understand that those Saints who lived in the transition time did not have salvation, justification, or eternal life in its consummated form. Notice what [*Apostle*] Paul says:

Philippians 3:12

Not that I have already attained, or am already perfected; but I press on, that I may lay hold of that for which Christ Jesus has also laid hold of me.

What was it that [*Apostle*] Paul had not yet attained? The Greek word used here for "attained" is *lambano*. It means: "to receive, to grasp, to seize, to acquire." [*Apostle*] Paul is saying, "I don't have it yet." What is it that he doesn't have yet? The verb *lambano* is transitive, but the object is not expressed. Is it the resurrection that he mentioned in verse 11 that he has not attained? Yes, the resurrection is included, but it is more than that, Philippians 3:4-11 are a unit speaking of justification. The key verse being:

Philippians 3:9

and be found in Him, not having my own righteousness, which is from the law, but that which is through faith in Christ, the righteousness which is from God by faith;

I think that what [*Apostle*] Paul is saying is that his **justification** had not yet been consummated. That would mean that eternal life had not been consummated. That might not fit your theology, but it fits the context of what [*Apostle*] Paul has been talking about. [*Apostle*] Paul was saying, "**Not that I have already attained, or have already been justified.**"

Jesus Christ took our sin and bore its penalty on the cross, and He gives us His righteousness.

2 Corinthians 5:21

For He made Him who knew no sin to be sin for us, that we might become the righteousness of God in Him.

We have been declared righteous by God for all eternity. It will never be reversed or changed. Christ's righteousness has been imputed to our account. Justification involves the imputation of Christ's righteousness. But at the time of [*Apostle*] Paul's writing, righteousness was still a hope. Now, you might ask, "Didn't [*Apostle*] Paul and the New Testament Saints already have the righteousness of God?" Yes and no. The futuristic perspective of God's righteousness was clearly expressed by [*Apostle*] Paul.

Galatians 5:5

For we through the Spirit eagerly wait for the hope of righteousness by faith.

If righteousness was already a fulfilled or completed event, [*Apostle*] Paul made a big mistake in making "righteousness" by faith a matter of hope. You don't hope for what you have.

Romans 8:24-25

For we were saved in this hope, but hope that is seen is not hope; for why does one still hope for what he sees? But if we hope for what we do not see, we eagerly wait for it with perseverance.

If righteousness were a present reality, why would [*Apostle*] Paul hope for it? But [*Apostle*] Paul also talks as though it was a present possession.

Romans 4:5

But to him who does not work but believes on Him who justifies the ungodly, his faith is accounted for righteousness,

Did [*Apostle*] Paul have Christ's righteousness or was it still future to him? Yes! He had it, but it was also still future to him. How can this be?

[*Apostle*] Paul lived in what the Bible calls the "last days"—they were the last days of the Old Covenant. Those "last days" began at the time of Christ and ended at AD 70 when the Jewish temple was destroyed. We now live in what the Bible calls **"the age to come,"** which is the New Covenant age. The forty-year period, from Pentecost to Holocaust, was a time of **transition** from the Old Covenant to the New Covenant. In this transition period, the New Covenant had been inaugurated but not consummated. It was a time of **"ALREADY BUT NOT YET."**

Galatians 5:5

*For we through the Spirit **eagerly wait** for the hope of righteousness by faith.* (Emphasis Author's)

The words translated: "*eagerly wait*" are the Greek word *apekdechomai*. This Greek word is only used seven times in the New Testament, and every one of them is in reference to the "Second Coming". Thus, righteousness comes at the "Second Coming".

Salvation was not a completed event in the lives of the First Century Believers, it was their hope, they looked forward to its soon arrival.

Romans 13:11-12

*And do this, knowing the time, that now it is high time to awake out of sleep; for **NOW OUR SALVATION IS NEARER** than when we first believed. The night is far spent, the day is at hand. Therefore let us cast off the works of darkness, and let us put on the armor of light.* (Emphasis Author's)

He equates their salvation with the "day" which was at hand, referring to the day of the Lord. *"Knowing the time"* is the Greek word *kairos*, it means: "season, a special critical strategic period of time." It is used of a season of great importance in redemptive history. The completion of redemptive history was at hand, and with it would come salvation.

[*Apostle*] Peter also states that their salvation was not yet complete:
1 Peter 1:5

who are kept by the power of God through faith for salvation ready to be revealed in the last time.

Salvation was ready to be revealed, when? In the last time, which would happen at the "*Second Coming of Christ*".
1 Peter 1:7

that the genuineness of your faith, being much more precious than gold that perishes, though it is tested by fire, may be found to praise, honor, and glory at the revelation of Jesus Christ,

In this same way, **"eternal life"** was not a present possession, but a hope. Please remember the "already but not yet" character of the transition period. They had eternal life positionally, but it would not be theirs in fact until the Lord returned.
Titus 3:5-7

not by works of righteousness which we have done, but according to His mercy He saved us, through the washing of regeneration and renewing of the Holy Spirit, whom He poured out on us abundantly through Jesus Christ our Savior, that having been justified by His grace we should become heirs according to **THE HOPE OF ETERNAL LIFE**. (Emphasis Author's)

Again, you don't hope for what you already have.
Jude 1:21

keep yourselves in the love of God, looking for the mercy of our Lord Jesus Christ unto eternal life.

The NIV makes this verse much clearer:
Jude 1:21

Keep yourselves in God's love as you wait for the mercy of our Lord Jesus Christ to bring you to eternal life. NIV

They had the hope of eternal life (already), but they did not have it as a present possession (not yet). Eternal life was something that was to come to them at the "Second Coming", in the "age to come."
Mark 10:29-31

So Jesus answered and said, "Assuredly, I say to you, there is no one who has left house or brothers or sisters or father or mother or wife or children or lands, for My sake and the gospel's, who shall not receive a hundredfold **NOW IN THIS TIME**; *houses and brothers and sisters and mothers and children and lands, with persecutions; and* **IN THE AGE TO COME, ETERNAL LIFE**. *But many who are first will be last, and the last first."* (Emphasis Author's)

Eternal life was a condition of the age to come!

The incompleteness of Believers during the transition period, 30-70 AD, does not contradict [*Apostle*] Paul's affirmation, *"Ye are complete in Him"* (Colossians 2:10). The certain completeness of Christ's work was the basis and confidence of the transformation already at work, with the future fullness drawing near.

I think that it is safe to say that most Believers think redemption was completed at the cross. But this is not what the Bible teaches; redemption is tied to the "Second Coming".

Luke 21:27-28

Then they will see the Son of Man coming in a cloud with power and great glory. "Now when these things begin to happen, look up and lift up your heads, because your redemption draws near."

When Christ returned, He brought redemption. As long as the Old Covenant existed, the Believers were not perfect and did not have access to God.

Hebrews 9:8-10

*the Holy Spirit indicating this, that **THE WAY INTO THE HOLIEST OF ALL WAS NOT YET MADE MANIFEST WHILE THE FIRST TABERNACLE WAS STILL STANDING**. It was symbolic for the **present time** in which both gifts and sacrifices are offered which cannot make him who performed the service **PERFECT** in regard to the conscience; concerned only with foods and drinks, various washings, and fleshly ordinances imposed **until the time of reformation**. (Emphasis Author's)*

Under the Old Covenant, they were never made perfect. And because they were not perfect, they could not enter God's presence. The incompleteness of what they had is seen in the fact that even though they had eternal life, they still needed to be raised up at the last day.

John 6:40

And this is the will of Him who sent Me, that everyone who sees the Son and believes in Him may have everlasting life; and I will raise him up at the last day.

John 6:44

No one can come to Me unless the Father who sent Me draws him; and I will raise him up at the last day.

John 6:54

Whoever eats My flesh and drinks My blood has eternal life, and I will raise him up at the last day.

Remember, resurrection is: "being brought into the presence of God."
What the Saints had in the transition period was the down payment of the perfection that was to come.
Ephesians 1:13-14

In Him you also trusted, after you heard the word of truth, the gospel of your salvation; in whom also, having believed, you were sealed with the Holy Spirit of promise, **WHO IS THE GUARANTEE OF OUR INHERITANCE UNTIL THE REDEMPTION OF THE PURCHASED POSSESSION**, *to the praise of His glory.* (Emphasis Author's)

The word "guarantee" is the Greek word *arrhabon*, which means: "a pledge, i.e. part of the purchase-money or property given in advance as security for the rest: earnest." We see this same idea in the following verses of Scripture:
2 Corinthians 1:22

who also has sealed us and given us the Spirit in our hearts as a guarantee.

2 Corinthians 5:5

Now He who has prepared us for this very thing is God, who also has given us the Spirit as a guarantee.

The transition Saints had in pledge what we now have. They had a guarantee of what was to come. We have it all.
Well, if the transition Saints did not go to Heaven, then what does [*Apostle*] Paul mean in the following?

2 Corinthians 5:8

We are confident, yes, well pleased rather to be absent from the body and to be present with the Lord.

Philippians 1:23

For I am hard pressed between the two, having a desire to depart and be with Christ, which is far better.

I think that if you study the context of these two verses, you will see that [*Apostle*] Paul was talking about himself in the Philippians passage and in the Corinthian passage the "we" most likely refers to [*Apostles*] Paul, Timothy and Silas. I submit that what [*Apostle*] Paul is saying here is that if he or his companions died, they would go directly to Heaven. [*Remember they were living at a very hostile period at the beginning of this New Covenant Church and many of them were killed, or became martyrs*].

Could [*Apostle*] Paul go to Heaven apart from the resurrection? No, but [*Apostle*] Paul knew that if he died for the witness of Christ and the word of God, he would be part of the **first resurrection.** During the transition period, those Believers who died a martyr's death were part of the **first resurrection.** Look with me at Revelation 20.

Revelation 20:4

And I saw thrones, and they sat on them, and judgment was committed to them. Then I saw the **SOULS OF THOSE WHO HAD BEEN BEHEADED FOR THEIR WITNESS TO JESUS AND FOR THE WORD OF GOD**, *who had not worshiped the beast or his image, and had not received his mark on their foreheads or on their hands. And* **THEY LIVED AND REIGNED WITH CHRIST FOR A THOUSAND YEARS**. (Emphasis Author's)

These are clearly martyred Believers from the transition period. They didn't worship the beast or take his number.

Revelation 20:5

But the rest of the dead did not live again until the thousand years were finished. This is the first resurrection.

No matter what your theological persuasion, there is a problem in this verse. If those of verse 4 lived and reigned with Christ for a thousand years, then how can those of verse 5 be the first resurrection? [*I submit*] They can't be. [*I submit*] The simple solution here is to see that they put the verse number in the wrong place. Verse 5 is a parenthesis that he will take up later in the chapter. [*Again, I submit that*] It should read like this: [*see if you agree*]

Revelation 20:5

But the rest of the dead did not live again until the thousand years were finished.

So the martyrs lived and reigned with Christ during the transition period (the thousand years) but the rest of the dead, everyone else who died, did not live again until the end of the transition period. [*Then*] Let's leave verse 5 out and read from 4 to 6. [*See if you agree*]

Revelation 20:4,6

And I saw thrones, and they sat on them, and judgment was committed to them. Then I saw the souls of those who had been beheaded for their witness to Jesus and for the word of God, who had not worshiped the beast or his image, and had not received his mark on their foreheads or on their hands. And they lived and reigned with Christ for a thousand years. . . .. This is the first resurrection. Blessed and holy is he who has part in the first resurrection. Over such the second death has no power, but they shall be priests of God and of Christ, and shall reign with Him a thousand years.

So, the martyrs of the transition period went to Heaven as part of the first resurrection. But everyone else went at the general resurrection at the end of the age. These first resurrection martyrs went to Heaven, but they were not in the Holiest of all, the presence of God, until the Temple was destroyed in [*circa*] AD 70.

Hebrews 9:8

> *the Holy Spirit indicating this, that the way into the Holiest of All was not yet made manifest while the first tabernacle was still standing.*

Then at [*circa*] AD 70, when Christ returned, the Believers in Hades (Old Testament Saints and transition Saints) were resurrected into the presence of God, and those in Heaven went into the presence of God.

When [*Apostle*] Paul was comforting the Thessalonians about their deceased loved ones, notice what he said: 1 Thessalonians 4:13-17

> *But I do not want you to be ignorant, brethren, concerning those who have* **FALLEN ASLEEP**, *lest you sorrow as others who have no hope. For if we believe that Jesus died and rose again, even so God will bring with Him those who sleep in Jesus. For this we say to you by the word of the Lord, that we who are alive and remain until the coming of the Lord will by no means precede* **THOSE WHO ARE ASLEEP**. *For the Lord Himself will descend from heaven with a shout, with the voice of an archangel, and with the trumpet of God.* **AND THE DEAD IN CHRIST WILL RISE FIRST**. *Then we who are alive and remain shall be caught up together with them in the clouds to meet the Lord in the air. And thus we shall always be with the Lord.* (Emphasis Author's)

[*Apostle*] Paul doesn't say, "Don't worry about your loved ones who recently died, they're in Heaven. Remember what I taught you, 'to be absent from the body is to be present with the Lord.'" What [*Apostle*] Paul did say was at the "Second Coming" their dead loved ones would "rise," they would be resurrected.

Believers since [*circa*] AD 70, have immortality.

1 Corinthians 15:51-54

> *Behold, I tell you a mystery: We shall not all sleep, but we shall all be changed; in a moment, in the twinkling of an eye, at the last trumpet.*

For the trumpet will sound, and **THE DEAD WILL BE RAISED INCORRUPTIBLE, AND WE SHALL BE CHANGED***. For this corruptible must put on incorruption, and this mortal must put on immortality. So when this corruptible has put on incorruption, and this mortal has put on immortality, then shall be brought to pass the saying that is written: "Death is swallowed up in victory.* (Emphasis Author's)

When Christ returned with the sound of the trumpet, the dead were raised, and the living were changed. All Believers put on immortality, and death was swallowed up—no more Hades.

Believers, we are no longer living in the "already but not yet" of the transition period. We are living in the New Covenant age in which righteousness dwells. We are not living in the age of "hope," we are living in the age of **"have."** The righteousness of Christ is ours; eternal life is ours, and immortality is ours. For us, to be absent from the body is to be present with the Lord.

For someone to believe that Christ has not yet returned and yet believe that Christians go to Heaven when they die is to be very inconsistent. Nobody goes to Heaven apart from the resurrection. Again, remember that this was spoken/written over 2000 years ago. This is fulfilled history. When we today die, we go directly to Heaven, to be with the Lord, we do not have to wait, because to be *absent from the body is to be present with the Lord.*

Luke 14:12-13

Then He also said to him who invited Him, "When you give a dinner or a supper, do not ask your friends, your brothers, your relatives, nor rich neighbours, lest they also invite you back, and you be repaid. But when you give a feast, invite the poor, the maimed, the lame, the blind."

Matthew 5:11-12

Blessed are you when they revile and persecute you, and say all kinds of evil against you falsely for My sake. "Rejoice and be exceedingly glad, for great is your reward in heaven, for so they persecuted the prophets who were before you."

"Your reward in Heaven" is the same as "you shall be repaid at the resurrection of the just." When you are resurrected, you go to Heaven, and not until. If Christ has not come and the resurrection has not happened, then all those who died in Christ are in Sheol.

In the following chapter we would once again look at another teaching from Pastor David B. Curtis of the Berean Bible Church at 1000 Chattanooga Street, Chesapeake, VA 23322, USA that continues to bring much light to our understanding of what the Bible teaches concerning death and the resurrection. He deals with Daniel 12 and this was delivered on March 27, 2016. For more of his teachings you can visit them at the following address: http://www.bereanbiblechurch.org/studies/eschatology.php

CHAPTER FOUR
DANIEL ON THE RESURRECTION

THE SINGLE MOST SIGNIFICANT EVENT IN THE HISTORY OF THE HUMAN RACE took place on the first Sunday after Passover in about the year A.D. 30. It was the resurrection of Yeshua [*Jesus Christ*]. He overcame the grave, He defeated death, and He promises resurrection life to all who trust in Him.

Futurists say—The Resurrection of Believers will happen sometime in the future, but Preterists say that it happened in the past. What does the Bible say? In this writing we are going to look at what Daniel says about the timing of The Resurrection. Let's look at Daniel 12 and see what it tells us about the time of The Resurrection: [All quotes unless otherwise stated are taken from the North American Standard Bible [NASB]]

Daniel 12:1

> *Now at that time Michael, the great prince who stands guard over the sons of your people, will arise. And there will be a time of distress such as never occurred since there was a nation until that time; and at that time your people, everyone who is found written in the book, will be rescued.*

"*Now at that time*"—since we jumped in at chapter 12, we don't have a clue as to what time "that time" is unless we look back at the previous chapters. So, let's go back to Daniel 10:

Daniel 10:14

Now I have come to give you an understanding of what will happen to your people in the latter days, for the vision pertains to the days yet future.

Here Daniel is being given a vision of what will happen to *"your people"* (the Israelites) in the latter days. This vision is of the future, it is of the last days of Israel:
Daniel 11:40

At the end time the king of the South will collide with him, and the king of the North will storm against him with chariots, with horsemen and with many ships; and he will enter countries, overflow them and pass through.

The *"at that time"* of chapter 12 is the *"latter days"* of 10:14, and the *"end time"* of chapter 11. So, Daniel 12 is talking about the "end times," which we know is referring to the end of the Old Covenant dispensation.

"Michael, the great prince"—who is this great Prince Michael who stands guard over Daniel's people? The name Michael is from the Hebrew *Miykael,* and means: "(one) who is like God." We see Michael three times in the *Tanakh:*
Daniel 10:13

But the prince of the kingdom of Persia was withstanding me for twenty-one days; then behold, Michael, one of the chief princes, came to help me, for I had been left there with the kings of Persia.

The context here demands that this "prince" be considered a supernatural being rather than a royal human individual. The literature from *Qumran* also uses the title "prince" as a reference to chief angels. Jude calls Michael the archangel, which means: "chief of the angels." (Jude 1:9)

I believe that this prince of the kingdom of Persia is the deity given custody of Persia when the 70 nations were divided up among the watchers in Genesis 10. In the Book of Sirach, which is part of what is considered the Apocrypha and appears in the Catholic Bible, it says: *"He appointed a ruler for every nation, but Israel is the Lord's own portion."* (Sirach 17:17) That is what Deuteronomy 32:8-9 teaches.

We see this prince of Persia battling with Michael who is one of the chief princes:

Daniel 10:21

However, I will tell you what is inscribed in the writing of truth. Yet there is no one who stands firmly with me against these forces except Michael your prince.

Again, we see Michael called a prince. The only other use of Michael in the *Tanakh* is in our text in Daniel 12:

Daniel 12:1

Now at that time Michael, the great prince who stands guard over the sons of your people, will arise. And there will be a time of distress such as never occurred since there was a nation until that time; and at that time your people, everyone who is found written in the book, will be rescued.

Here we see that Michael is the "great prince" who stands guard over Daniel's people. Michael is the patron archangel of Israel. Michael is depicted as warring on behalf of Israel and is called "Israel's protector." This is one of Yahweh's council members; this is a high-ranking celestial being. So, in Daniel 10 we see two of the gods battling over Israel. The prince of the Kingdom of Persia and Michael the prince.

When we come to the New Testament, we see Michael again battling a prince, but now it is satan:

Revelation 12:7

And there was war in heaven, Michael and his angels waging war with the dragon. The dragon and his angels waged war,

What nation is satan the prince over? Rome! satan is the spiritual power behind Rome (the beast). We saw in Daniel that Persia and Greece had a "prince" or Watcher behind them (in Daniel 10). Wouldn't it make sense that a Watcher or chief angel would be behind Rome also? And that is exactly what the book of Revelation presents. The beast represents Rome and the dragon that gives power to the beast is satan. There are some who believe that Michael is the pre-incarnate Christ. I argued for this view in the past. But notice here the word:

Daniel 10:13

But the prince of the kingdom of Persia was withstanding me for twenty-one days; then behold, Michael, one of the chief princes, came to help me, for I had been left there with the kings of Persia.

"Princes" is plural; how can there be more than one chief prince if Michael is Christ Himself? Who are the other chief princes? Some try to argue that this plural "princes" is a reference to the trinity. But that's not a good argument.

In Jewish tradition, Michael is the leader of archangels who dwell in the presence of God (Ascension of Isaiah 3:16). In this capacity, he functions in a number of roles. He is "the patron angel of Israel. . . . fighting for Israel" against her enemies; he is "an intercessor for Israel before God."

The very fact that Michael is described as an archangel indicates that there are different ranks or orders of angels. In other apocryphal books the number of archangels is given as 7 (Enoch 20:1-7; Tobit 12:15).

Daniel 12 goes on to call Michael, **"The great prince who stands guard over the sons of your people, will arise"**—we know that the sons of "your people" is a reference to the Hebrew people. Here Michael is the great prince that stands guard over the Israelites.

"And there will be a time of distress such as never occurred since there was a nation until that time"—now remember that this is to happen "at that time," which is referring to the end of the Jewish age. So, Daniel is predicting a time of great trouble in Israel at the end of the age. Daniel tells us that during this time of distress some of his people will be rescued. Jeremiah tells us the same thing:

Jeremiah 30:4-7

Now these are the words which the LORD spoke concerning Israel and concerning Judah: "For thus says the LORD, 'I have heard a sound of terror, Of dread, and there is no peace. Ask now, and see If a male can give birth. Why do I see every man With his hands on his loins, as a woman in childbirth? And why have all faces turned pale? 'Alas! for that day is great, There is none like it; And it is the time of Jacob's distress, But he will be saved from it.'"

Jeremiah is talking about a time of trouble and says, *"There is none like it."* Then he says that this same time period of great distress is a time in which some will be saved. Yeshua [*Jesus Christ*] also talked about this time. In Matthew 24 Yeshua [*Jesus Christ*] is answering the disciples' questions about the destruction of Jerusalem. They wanted to know when it would be destroyed, and what signs would precede the end of the age and His Parousia:

Matthew 24:21

For then there will be a great tribulation, such as has not occurred since the beginning of the world until now, nor ever will.

Yeshua [*Jesus Christ*], talking to Jews, tells them, *"'then' there will be great tribulation."* The "then" is referring to the context of verses 15-20; when you see the abomination of desolation, which Luke tells us is Jerusalem surrounded by armies. This happened in A.D. 67 when Cestius Gallus, the Roman general, laid siege to Jerusalem. The Great Tribulation is not an event yet future to us. It was "then," during the siege of Jerusalem by the Romans in the First Century. This is made abundantly clear in the parallel text in Luke's Gospel:

Luke 21:20-22

But when you see Jerusalem surrounded by armies, then recognize that her desolation is near. "Then those who are in Judea must flee to the mountains, and those who are in the midst of the city must leave, and those who are in the country must not enter the city; because these are days of vengeance, so that all things which are written will be fulfilled."

Luke tells us here that ALL things which, are written will be fulfilled in the destruction of Jerusalem. What does he mean by that? *"All things which are written"* refers to prophecy. All prophecy was to be fulfilled in the destruction of Jerusalem. Daniel tells us about this very same thing in:

Daniel 9:24

Seventy weeks have been decreed for your people and your holy city, to finish the transgression, to make an end of sin, to make atonement for iniquity, to bring in everlasting righteousness, to seal up vision and prophecy and to anoint the most holy place.

Daniel was told that 70 weeks had been determined on his people Israel and city Jerusalem. The Hebrew word used here for *"have been decreed"* is *chatha*, which literally means: "to cut off." The 70 weeks is symbolic. By the end of this prophetic time period, God promised that six things would be accomplished. One of the things that Daniel was told would happen by the end of that period was that God would *"seal up vision and prophecy."* The Hebrew commentaries agree on the meaning of to "seal up vision and prophecy"—they say it means: "the end and complete fulfillment of all prophecy."

Daniel's prophecy, then, tells of the time when all prophecy would cease to be given, and what had been given would be fulfilled. When would this be? Daniel's vision begins with the decree to rebuild Jerusalem and ends with the destruction of Jerusalem, which we know occurred in A.D. 70.

The fall of Jerusalem was far more than the fall of a city; it was the end of an age. That is why Yeshua [Jesus Christ] said it would be a, *"great tribulation, such as has not been since the beginning of the world until this time, no, nor ever shall be."*

For this reason, I ask, "How could it be possible for there to be in the future a destruction of Jerusalem equal or greater than that which happened in A.D. 70?" Yeshua [Jesus Christ] said nothing in time would ever equal what happened in A.D. 70, nothing.

I'm sorry to have to tell you that the Great Tribulation is behind us, it is an event in history. Though most of the Church looks for it to happen in the future; it is past. You missed it; I hope you are not too disappointed.

Let's go back to Matthew and notice what he says in the next verse:
Matthew 24:22

Unless those days had been cut short, no life would have been saved; but for the sake of the elect those days will be cut short.

This is the same thing we saw in Daniel 12:1, *"And at that time your people, everyone who is found written in the book, will be rescued"*—So Daniel, Jeremiah, and Yeshua [*Jesus Christ*] all talk about this same time of great tribulation when Yahweh will save His people. Yeshua [*Jesus Christ*] tells us exactly when this time was to be:

Matthew 24:34

Truly I say to you, this generation will not pass away until all these things take place.

Yeshua [*Jesus Christ*] here, very plainly and very clearly, tells HIS DISCIPLES that ALL of the things He had mentioned would come to pass in THEIR GENERATION. This includes the Gospel being preached in all the world, the Abomination of Desolation, the Great Tribulation, and the Coming of the Son of man. This is so clear that it greatly troubles those who hold to a Futuristic Eschatology.

Yeshua [*Jesus Christ*] uses the near demonstrative "this" generation. Every time "this" is used in the New Testament it always refers to something that is near in terms of time or distance. Yeshua [*Jesus Christ*] could have said, "That generation." But He didn't! Yeshua [*Jesus Christ*] is saying that everything that He has spoken about will happen before the generation that He was speaking to would pass away.

So Daniel is talking about a time that the generation that Yeshua [*Jesus Christ*] lived in would see all these things fulfilled. **"And at that time your people, everyone who is found written in the book, will be rescued"**—the "your people" here are Daniel's people, who would be Israelites. At the time of The Great Tribulation all the Israelites that are found in the book will be rescued. So during the time of The Great Tribulation the elect of Yahweh would be delivered from that tribulation. How did this happen? Notice what Yeshua [*Jesus Christ*] told His disciples:

Matthew 24:15-21

Therefore when you see the ABOMINATION OF DESOLATION which was spoken of through Daniel the prophet, standing in the holy place (let the reader understand), then those who are in Judea must flee to the mountains. "Whoever is on the housetop must not go down to get the things out that are in his house. Whoever is in the field must not turn back to get his cloak. But woe to those who are pregnant and to those who are nursing babies in those days! But pray that your flight will not be in the winter, or on a Sabbath. For then there will be a great tribulation, such as has not occurred since the beginning of the world until now, nor ever will."

So, when they saw the armies surrounding Jerusalem, they were to flee. They were to get out before the tribulation began. It is a historical fact that Cestius Gallus, the Roman general, for some unknown reason, suspended the siege against Jerusalem, ceased the attack and withdrew his armies for an interval of time after the Romans had occupied the Temple, thus giving every Believer the opportunity to obey the Lord's instruction to flee the city.

Josephus, the eyewitness, himself an unbeliever, chronicles this fact, and admitted his inability to account for the cessation of the fighting at this time after a siege had begun. We can account for it. Yahweh was giving His people, believing Israelites, a chance to escape the siege, and the disciples took it. And just as Daniel 12:1 had said, **"everyone who is found written in the book, will be rescued."** Daniel said it, Jeremiah said it, Yeshua [*Jesus Christ*] said it. And it happened exactly as was predicted.

Now, notice the next verse in Daniel 12:

Daniel 12:2

Many of those who sleep in the dust of the ground will awake, these to everlasting life, but the others to disgrace and everlasting contempt.

This is The Resurrection of the just and the unjust. Now remember that this is in the context of verse 1, the time of Great Tribulation in the end time or last days of Israel, which ended in A.D. 70. This Resurrection happens after the time of Jerusalem's destruction, not at the end of time as most Believers think. Most Christians think that The Resurrection is a yet future event. Notice what Daniel says next:

Daniel 12:3

Those who have insight will shine brightly like the brightness of the expanse of heaven, and those who lead the many to righteousness, like the stars forever and ever.

So, after The Resurrection we have people who are turning many to righteousness. How could this be if The Resurrection was at the end of time? Who are those who shine brightly like the brighteners of the expanse of Heaven? This is astral language to speak of Believers.

They viewed the stars as deities.

Job 38:7

When the morning stars sang together And all the sons of God shouted for joy?

Here "stars" and "sons of God" are synonymous. Daniel is saying that Believers in The Resurrection will be like the sons of God, we will be like stars. This is what Yahweh promised Abram in Genesis 15:

Genesis 15:5

And He took him outside and said, "Now look toward the heavens, and count the stars, if you are able to count them." And He said to him, "So shall your descendants be."

The CJB (Complete Jewish Bible) puts it this way:

Genesis 15:5

Then he brought him outside and said, "Look up at the sky, and count the stars — if you can count them! Your descendants will be that many!" CJB

The question here is does, *"So shall your descendants be"* refer only to the quantitative—you'll be as numerous as the stars, or does it refer qualitatively—you will be like stars? I think it is both. This is *theosis*, "the deification of man." We are to be like the divine host, part of Yahweh's celestial family.

What we have in Daniel 12:3 is astral in nature and language. This text reads The Resurrection in astral terms, *"in the resurrection they will shine as the stars of heaven."*

And in Daniel 12 we see this happening after The Resurrection, so when does The Resurrection take place?

Daniel 12:13

But as for you, go your way to the end; then you will enter into rest and rise again for your allotted portion at the end of the age.

According to this verse, when is The Resurrection to take place? It is to take place at, "the end of the age." There are only two ages talked about in the Bible, "this age," which was the Old Covenant age, and "the age to come," which was the New Covenant age, the age in which we live. The New Covenant has no last days, no end time; so, the end of the age must refer to the end of the Old Covenant. There is no newer covenant to end the New Covenant.

Notice what Yeshua [*Jesus Christ*] says in Matthew 13:
Matthew 13:41-43

The Son of Man will send forth His angels, and they will gather out of His kingdom all stumbling blocks, and those who commit lawlessness, and will cast them into the furnace of fire; in that place there shall be weeping and gnashing of teeth. "Then THE RIGHTEOUS WILL SHINE FORTH AS THE SUN in the kingdom of their Father. He who has ears, let him hear."

Yeshua [*Jesus Christ*] tells us that at the end of the age the lawless will be cast into a furnace of fire and will be weeping and gnashing their teeth. This is The Great Tribulation that Daniel talks about. Then he says, *"The righteousness will shine forth as the sun"* quoting Daniel 12:3. So all this stuff: The Great Tribulation, The Resurrection, and the righteous shining forth as the sun all happens at the end of the Jewish age. Both Daniel 12 and Matthew 13 are speaking about the destruction of Jerusalem in A.D. 70. The Resurrection is an event that was to happen in A.D. 70.

Since we know that The Resurrection is past, we know that it was spiritual and not physical. The Resurrection of the dead that took place at the end of the Old Covenant in A.D. 70 was not a biological resurrection of dead decayed bodies, it was a release from Sheol of all who had been waiting through the centuries to be reunited with God in the Heavenly Kingdom.

We can see from the teaching of Hymenaeus and Philetus several things about The Resurrection beliefs of the early Christians:
2 Timothy 2:17-18

and their talk will spread like gangrene. Among them are Hymenaeus and Philetus, men who have gone astray from the truth saying that the resurrection has already taken place, and they upset the faith of some.

The early Christians must have believed that The Resurrection would be spiritual in nature, and, therefore, not subject to confirmation by any physical evidence. If the early Christians had believed that The Resurrection would involve the physical bodies coming out of the graves, as is taught today, Hymenaius and Philitus could never have convinced anyone that The Resurrection had already happened.

They also must have believed that life on earth would go on with no material change after The Resurrection. They didn't believe that they would be on a renovated planet earth as a consequence of The Resurrection. Otherwise, the teaching of Hymenaeus and Philetus would have been impossible. No one would have paid any attention to them.

The reason that their teaching that The Resurrection had already happened was overthrowing the faith of some was that it postulated a consummation of the spiritual kingdom, while the earthly Temple in Jerusalem still stood. This was a mixture of Law and grace. This destroyed the faith of some by making the works of the Law a part of the New Covenant.

Daniel 12:4

*But as for you, Daniel, conceal these words and seal up the book **until the end of time**; many will go back and forth, and knowledge will increase.* (Emphasis Author's)

Daniel is to seal up the book until when. *"The end of time."* **This is a very bad translation**. Young's Literal Translation translates this as, *"the time of the end."* The KJV and even the NIV translate it that way also. We know that this should not be translated "end of time" if we look at verse 7:

Daniel 12:7

I heard the man dressed in linen, who was above the waters of the river, as he raised his right hand and his left toward heaven, and swore by Him who lives forever that it would be for a time, times, and half a time; and as soon as they finish shattering the power of the holy people, all these events will be completed.

Notice the end of this verse, *"as soon as they finish shattering the power of the holy people, all these events will be completed."* All what events will be completed?

- The Great Tribulation in verse 1
- The Resurrection in verse 2
- Many being turned to righteousness in verse 3
- And the shattering of the power of the holy people

So, all these events will be completed when the power of the holy people is shattered. So, when does that happen? Is it at the end of time as verse 4 says? Who are the holy people? In context it is Daniel's people, which are the Israelites. So, when was it that the Israelites' power was completely shattered? It was during the great tribulation when the Temple and the city of Jerusalem were destroyed.

Since the tribulation did not happen at the end of time, but at the end of the Old Covenant age, we know that the NASB translation "end of time" in Daniel 12:4, is wrong. Let me just say here that the Bible does not speak of "**the end of time**." The expression "the end time" or the "time of the end" is found in Scripture, but nowhere in the Bible can we find the expression "the end of time." The expression "the end time" or the "time of the end" speaks of the end of an age, but the end of an age is not the end of time. Scripture does not indicate that God has any plan to destroy this created world that we enjoy. Here are a couple of Bible verses that support this thought, from the King James Version:

Isaiah 45:17

But Israel shall be saved in the Lord with an everlasting salvation: ye shall not be ashamed nor confounded world without end.

Ephesians 3:21

Unto him be glory in the church by Christ Jesus throughout all ages, world without end. Amen.

Ok then, let's go back to the passage we were speaking about in the book of Daniel verse 4, but let us read it from the NKJV:
Daniel 12:4

*But you, Daniel, shut up the words, and seal the book until **the time of the end**; many shall run to and fro, and knowledge shall increase. Emphasis Author's*

Daniel is told to *"conceal these words and seal up the book until the time of the end."* These things were not going to be understood until the time of the end. When the end times arrived, Yeshua [*Jesus Christ*], referring to Daniels words, said:
Mark 13:14

But when you see the ABOMINATION OF DESOLATION standing where it should not be (let the reader understand), then let those who are in Judea flee to the mountains.

Mark adds, *"(let the reader understand)."* This is designed to draw the attention of the reader of Daniel to the passages' true meaning. In other words, when you see Jerusalem surrounded by armies, that is the sign of the destruction of Jerusalem, the sign of His Coming and the end of the age.
Daniel 12:9

He said, "Go your way, Daniel, for these words are concealed and sealed up until the end time."

Again, Daniel is told that these words are sealed until the end time, or the last days of Israel. We are told in Daniel 12:4 that this *"time of the end"* will be a time when *"knowledge will increase."* How many of you have heard this verse used to say that the knowledge here is science and technology, and that it refers to our time? This is not talking about the knowledge of science or technology. Remember this is talking about the end of the Jewish age.

When the Bible talks about knowledge, it is referring to the knowledge of Yahweh. Prior to Pentecost and the coming of the New Covenant the knowledge of Yahweh was limited to whom? Israel!

Romans 9:4

who are Israelites, to whom belongs the adoption as sons, and the glory and the covenants and the giving of the Law and the temple service and the promises,

Only Israel had the knowledge of Yahweh. But after Pentecost the knowledge of Yahweh began to go to the nations. This is the knowledge that Daniel was talking about—it was the knowledge of the Gospel, the knowledge of God in Christ. Paul was used of Yahweh in the last days to increase this knowledge:

2 Corinthians 4:6

For God, who said, "Light shall shine out of darkness," is the One who has shone in our hearts to give the Light of the knowledge of the glory of God in the face of Christ.

Here Paul calls the Gospel the *"Light of the knowledge of the glory of God in the face of Christ."* Paul lived in the last days, and he helped this knowledge to increase. This is what Daniel was talking about. In the last days knowledge would increase, the knowledge of the Gospel of our LORD Yeshua Ha'Moshiach [Jesus the Messiah].

Daniel 12:5-6

Then I, Daniel, looked and behold, two others were standing, one on this bank of the river and the other on that bank of the river. And one said to the man dressed in linen, who was above the waters of the river, "How long will it be until the end of these wonders?"

This question seems to be asked for the sake of Daniel. The end of these things is the "end" that has been talked about from Daniel 11:40 to

12:3, with all that shall happen in: The Great Tribulation, the salvation of the elect, the Resurrection, all of it. The answer to the question is in the next verse:
Daniel 12:7

I heard the man dressed in linen, who was above the waters of the river, as he raised his right hand and his left toward heaven, and swore by Him who lives forever that it would be for a time, times, and half a time; and as soon as they finish shattering the power of the holy people, all these events will be completed.

"All these events" includes The Resurrection of verse 2. Daniel is told that The Resurrection will be when the power of the holy people (the Jews) has been completely shattered. So, The Resurrection was to happen at the end of the Jewish age, the Old Covenant age. We know that this happened in A.D. 70 with the destruction of the Jewish Temple.
Daniel 12:8-9

As for me, I heard but could not understand; so I said, "My lord, what will be the outcome of these events?" He said, "Go your way, Daniel, for these words are concealed and sealed up until the end time."

That is, till the time comes, or draws near, that they shall be accomplished; until then they would not be clearly understood. Then in the book of Revelation we read:
Revelation 22:10

And he said to me, "Do not seal up the words of the prophecy of this book, for the time is near." NASB

What was sealed in Daniel is being revealed in Revelation.
Back to Daniel: Daniel 12:10-11

Many will be purged, purified and refined, but the wicked will act wickedly; and none of the wicked will understand, but those who have insight will understand. "From the time that the regular sacrifice is abolished and the abomination of desolation is set up, there will be 1,290 days."

From the time the Abomination of Desolation is set up, there will be 1,290 days. How many years is that? Three and a half, which is how long the war against Jerusalem lasted. Yeshua [*Jesus Christ*] referred to this in Matthew 24:15, in discussing the fall of Jerusalem.

Many commentators find an allusion to the standards of the Roman legions in the expression, "The Abomination of Desolation." The eagles were objects of worship to the soldiers. We know from Josephus that the attempt of a Roman general, Vitellius, in the reign of Tiberius, to march his troops through Judea was resisted by the Jewish authorities, on the ground that the idolatrous images on their ensigns would be a profanation of the Law.

By combining Matthew and Luke's statements with secular history, it is clear that Cestius Gallus and his Roman army were the Abomination of Desolation. It was fulfilled in A.D.66 when the Romans surrounded the city of Jerusalem.

S. Chrysostom wrote: "For this it seems to me that the Abomination of Desolation means the army by which the holy city of Jerusalem was made desolate." (*The Ante-Nicene Fathers*)

Daniel 12:13

But as for you, go your way to the end; then you will enter into rest and rise again for your allotted portion at the end of the age.

The statements of verses 1, 7, 11, and 12 tie The Resurrection to the time immediately following the destruction of Jerusalem in A.D. 70. Daniel was to arise at the end of the age when the power of the holy people was shattered. How can you take this Resurrection and separate it from the destruction of Jerusalem? How can you do it?

So, The Resurrection was a spiritual re-gathering of Yahweh's covenant people. The Resurrection of the dead that took place at the end of the Old Covenant in A.D. 70 was not a biological resurrection of dead decayed bodies, but a release from Sheol of all who had been waiting through the centuries to be reunited with God in the Heavenly Kingdom.

They were no longer separated from God (dead), they were now in His presence (alive).

For Believers who have lived since A.D. 70, we are resurrected when we trust in Christ. Yeshua [*Jesus Christ*] gives us spiritual life, which is a resurrection from our state of spiritual death:

Ephesians 2:5

even when we were dead in our transgressions, made us alive together with Christ (by grace you have been saved),

We have eternal life and can never die spiritually. Therefore, we don't need a resurrection. At death our bodies go to dust, and we go immediately to Heaven:

John 11:25-26

Jesus said to her, "I am the resurrection and the life; he who believes in Me will live even if he dies, and everyone who lives and believes in Me will never die. Do you believe this?"

Yeshua [*Jesus Christ*] is saying, "He who believes in me shall live [spiritually], even if he dies [physically], and everyone who lives [physically], and believes in Me, shall never die [spiritually]."

Two categories of Believers are discussed: those who would die before the resurrection, and those who would not. For those who died under the Old Covenant, He was The Resurrection, but for those who lived into the days of the New Covenant, He is the Life.

Under the New Covenant, there is no death, spiritually speaking. Where there is no death, there is no need of a resurrection. We have eternal life and can never die spiritually. Therefore, we don't need a resurrection. At death, we go immediately to Heaven. [End of section by Pastor David B. Curtis]

In the next chapter we would seek to explore and bring some measure of clarity as to what is meant by "**The Last Trumpet**" in Scripture. After all the resurrection is supposed to take place after this Trumpet is blown!

Chapter Five
THE LAST TRUMPET

All of life is connected to a Source. Take anything from a plant to any animal they are all connected to a source. And that source is the earth. As we go into this section, I would like to revisit something I wrote earlier in Chapter One:

Even though I have read the bible on several occasions before, I just **never saw this one verse before although I would have read it several times before**. It is found in the Psalms

PSALM 90:10

> *The days of our lives are* **seventy years**; *And* **if by reason of strength *they are eighty* years**, *Yet their boast is only labor and sorrow; For it is soon cut off, and we fly away. Emphasis Author's*

However, some say that our lives should be 120 years according to:

GENESIS 6:3

> *And the Lord said, My Spirit shall not strive with man forever, for he is indeed flesh;* **yet his days shall be one hundred and twenty years**. *Emphasis Author's*

Again, remember that this was God speaking about how evil humans had become. Let us just read the verses in context when He said this: Let us read **Genesis 6:1-13**

> *Now it came to pass, when men began to multiply on the face of the earth, and daughters were born to them, that the sons of God saw the daughters of men, that they were beautiful; and they took wives for themselves of all whom they chose. And the Lord said,* "<u>**My Spirit shall not strive with man forever, for he** *is* **indeed flesh; yet his days shall be one hundred and twenty years**</u>." *There were giants on the earth in those days, and also afterward, when the sons of God came in to the daughters of men and they bore children to them. Those were the mighty men who were of old, men of renown.* **Then the Lord saw that the wickedness of man** *was* **great in the earth, and** *that* **every intent of the thoughts of his heart** *was* **only evil continually.** **And the Lord was sorry that He had made man on the earth, and He was grieved in His heart. So the Lord said, "I will destroy man whom I have created from the face of the earth, both man and beast, creeping thing and birds of the air**, *for I am sorry that I have made them."* <u>**But Noah found grace in the eyes of the Lord**</u>. *This is the genealogy of Noah.* <u>**Noah was a just man, perfect in his generations. Noah walked with God**</u>. *And Noah begot three sons: Shem, Ham, and Japheth.* **The earth also was corrupt before God, and the earth was filled with violence. So God looked upon the earth, and indeed it was corrupt; for all flesh had corrupted their way on the earth**. *And God said to Noah,* "<u>**The end of all flesh has come before Me, for the earth is filled with violence through them; and behold, I will destroy them with the earth**</u>. (Emphasis Author's)

Hence the reason I do believe that God was giving mankind the opportunity to repent before the destruction of the earth. But Noah found Grace in the eyes of the Lord.

Now we are not sure how long it took Noah and his sons to build this Ark; but we do know this: that all three sons were alive and already had wives when construction started and that Shem was 98 years old when the flood occurred.

In Genesis 5:32

*And Noah was **five hundred years old**, and Noah begot Shem, Ham, and Japheth.* (Emphasis Author's)

And then In Genesis 7:6, we read:

*Noah was **six hundred years old** when the floodwaters were on the earth.* (Emphasis Author's)

These two passages suggest a time period of about 100 years between Noah receiving the instruction from God to build the Ark and the start of the Flood.

BACK TO GENESIS 6:3

My Spirit shall not strive with man forever, for he is indeed flesh; yet his days shall be one hundred and twenty years. Emphasis Author's

Now, I want to revisit the creation of the first human couple. Never saw this in this light before—Adam, and **not Eve** was created in Eden and then God chose a place in Eden and named it, **The Garden of Eden** and there He placed Adam [It is like Adam was created in BC, but after he was created he was then placed in the city of Vancouver to live. He is still in BC, but he is now specifically in Vancouver. I hope you understand this] and **then God created Eve in the Garden where Adam now lived**. Let us look a bit deeper into this.

This Garden in the original Hebrew text meant that it was a protected place. This was done because God knew what they would eventually do and as such needed to have this place protected.

LET US REVISIT THE ACCOUNT IN GENESIS 2:7-8, 15-23

And the Lord God formed man of the dust of the ground, and breathed into his nostrils the breath of life; and man became a living being. The Lord God planted a garden eastward in Eden, and there He put the man whom He had formed. (Emphasis Author's)

> **Then the Lord God took the man and put him in the garden of Eden to tend and keep it**. [_At this point Eve was not yet created_]. And the Lord God commanded the man, [_Adam, and not Eve, as she was not yet created_] saying, "Of every tree of the garden you may freely eat; but of the tree of the knowledge of good and evil you shall not eat, for in the day that you eat of it you shall surely die." And the Lord God said, "**It is not good that man should be alone**; I will make him a helper comparable to him." Out of the ground the Lord God formed every beast of the field and every bird of the air, and brought **them** to Adam to see what he would call them. And whatever Adam called each living creature, that **was** its name. So Adam gave names to all cattle, to the birds of the air, and to every beast of the field [_Here we see Adam doing all the initial work of naming all the animals God had created_]. But for Adam there was not found a helper comparable to him [clearly revealing to us that bestiality (having sex with animals) is a sin]. [_Now, the creation of Eve, in the protected realm of The Garden of Eden._] And the Lord God caused a deep sleep to fall on Adam, and he slept; and He took one of his ribs, and closed up the flesh in its place. Then the rib which the Lord God had taken from man He made into a woman, and He brought her to the man. And Adam said: "**This is now bone of my bones And flesh of my flesh; She shall be called Woman, Because she was taken out of Man.**" (Parenthesis and Emphasis Author's)

Now, remember that it was into the first man Adam, God breathed His breath into and he became alive with all his learning/information to live successfully. However, they sinned after Eve was created.

Now we have to understand and see how crafty the devil was/is, he first tempted Eve as I do believe that he knew that God did not specifically speak to her, nor did He initially breathe His Spirit into her but into the man Adam. Also the fact that he had dealt directly with God's Spirit in his rebellion, so he knew that he could not directly contend with God's Spirit that was released into Adam, so he decided that Eve would be tempted first and then he would let her get her husband to follow her and disobey God. satan is a sly, 'crafty' one! Yes he is!

Eve first sinned and I do believe that if Adam had not heeded to the voice of his wife, God's plan would have been altered, because it was into Adam God breathed and not directly into Eve. I believe she got God's Breath from the rib of Adam. So, Adam had to be enticed to also eat of that forbidden fruit, see Genesis 3:17. **So,** by disobeying God they were put out of that protected realm; The Garden of Eden and a flaming sword was set up to guard that protected realm. Let us see it again in the following passage:

GENESIS 3:22-24

> *Then the Lord God said, "Behold, the man has become like one of Us, to know good and evil. And now, lest he put out his hand and take also of the tree of life, and eat, and live forever"*—**therefore the Lord God sent him out of the garden of Eden to till the ground from which he was taken**. *So He drove out the man; [and in reality the woman as well] and He placed a Cherubim at the east of the Garden of Eden, and a flaming sword which turned every way, to guard the way to the tree of life.* (Emphasis Author's)

And as we all know death was introduced. As a matter, I do believe that death was introduced as an act of Mercy on God's part. Mankind had to be able to die so that God's plan of redemption could be implemented.

In the early days of earth man used to live very long, but their sinful lifestyle got worse and worse until God just could not take it anymore so He wiped out His creation and started over with Noah and his family. Eight souls to be exact and we began to see the life span of humans lessen.

Now, one of the things that we need to fully understand here is this—when we die we are like a seed falling into the earth which will germinate and create a future plant. However, when that seed dies and is resurrected it comes into life not as the planted seed but as a whole new dimension, a whole new transformation—it comes forth as a tree or whatever plant is in the DNA of the seed. Still though the fruit that it ends up bearing will have new seeds in it. So, wrapped up in the body of flesh, which serves as an outer garment resides a whole new creation, a brand new you. As a matter of fact, that is what the born-again experience does for us—it releases into us a new, living spirit so that when we die our bodies can be then clothed with this new "clothing" or "skin" from God. In essence we become truly SPIRITUAL...

The next section of this chapter is a brief section from Dr. John Noë's book "The Greater Jesus". He has given us some very good information concerning "the last trumpet," which I believe would be very beneficial to any serious Bible student.

"AT THE LAST TRUMPET ..." WHEN WAS ALL THIS TO OCCUR? LET'S LOCATE THE LAST TRUMPET IN SCRIPTURE.

It's the seventh trumpet in Revelation 10 and 11. In prophetic symbolism, an angel sounding a trumpet represents a voice, or message, from God. And that's exactly what the last trumpet is! It is the message from the heavenly host proclaiming, "the kingdom of the world has become the kingdom of our Lord and of his Christ, and he will reign for ever and ever" (Revelation 11:15).

The last trumpet has already sounded in human history, many times, but not everyone has heard or received it. It continues to sound for individuals as they personally receive the revelation of the greater Jesus.

The sounding of the last trumpet does not summon people to leave, but to reign on this earth in this life. *"And you have made them to be a kingdom and priests to serve God, and they will reign on earth"* (Revelation 5:10).

This is the same trumpet Jesus referred to when He said, *"And He will send forth his angels with a great trumpet and they will gather his elect from the four winds, from one end of the heavens to the other"* (Matthew 24:31, also see Zephaniah 3:20).

When we receive and appropriate the unveiling and revealing of the greater Jesus, we are changed instantaneously into kings and priests to rule and reign in the Kingdom of God. Quit trying to put this all off into the future. This is a powerful spiritual/physical reality, available then and there and here and now.

"The dead will be raised imperishable ..." Who are these dead? In the facet of resurrection reality we are exploring here, they are those who are physically alive, but not reigning and ruling with Christ.

As [Apostle] Paul said, *"I want to know Christ and the power of his resurrection ... and so, somehow, to attain to the resurrection of the dead"* (Philippians 3:10-11). When? In his earthly life. Once again, that is why he also admonished believers to *"Wake up, O sleeper, rise from the dead, and Christ will shine on you"* (Ephesians 5:14).

Earlier, [*Apostle*] Paul had written, *"Flesh and blood cannot inherit the Kingdom of God, nor does perishable inherit imperishable"* (1 Corinthians 15:50).

We keep trying to drag the flesh into the Kingdom; but the flesh is what holds us back from inheriting the Kingdom. Our flesh is perishable, but our spirit is imperishable. It is eternal.

1 Peter 1:23

For you have been born again, not of perishable seed, but of the imperishable, through the living and enduring word of God.

When we fully receive the revelation of the last trumpet, we are changed, i.e., transformed, not removed. We suddenly realize that we are eternal. Our bodies even change as we offer them to God as instruments of righteousness (Romans 6:13) and living sacrifices (Romans 12:1).

Of course, our physical bodies die, stay on earth, and return to dust. This human eventuality and divinely determined destiny does not change (Hebrews 9:27 *And as it is appointed for men to die once, but after this the judgment,*). But our spirits live forever, and postmortem, in new "spiritual bodies" that "God gives" (1 Corinthians 15:38, 44 *But God gives it a body as He pleases, and to each seed its own body... It is sown a natural body, it is raised a spiritual body. There is a natural body, and there is a spiritual body.*).

The reality of the last trumpet revelation is that if we have been made alive in Christ, we are immortal (2 Corinthians 5:4 *For we who are in this tent groan, being burdened, not because we want to be unclothed, but further clothed, that mortality may be swallowed up by life.*; Proverbs 12:28 *In the way of righteousness is life, And in its pathway there is no death.*).

And when we fully realize our immortality, we are changed. We look at everything differently; we don't get all worried about earthly things; we think and operate on a different plane.

We are *"caught up with them in the clouds to meet the Lord in the air"* (1 Thessalonians 4:17). *"Death has been swallowed up in victory ..."* Christ, by his resurrection, has destroyed death as a universal fact. It's a done deal (2 Timothy 1:10 *but has now been revealed by the appearing of our Savior Jesus Christ, who has abolished death and brought life and immortality to light through the gospel*; Romans 8:2 *For the law of the Spirit of life in Christ Jesus has made me free from the law of sin and death.*; Revelation 21:4, 6 *And God will wipe away every tear from their eyes; there shall be no more death, nor sorrow, nor crying. There shall be no more pain, for the former things have passed away. And He said to me, "It is done! I am the Alpha and the Omega, the Beginning and the End. I will give of the fountain of the water of life freely to him who thirsts.*). Therefore, when we are co-resurrected in and with Him, individually, death is destroyed for us (John 8:51 *Most assuredly, I say to you, if anyone keeps My word he shall never see death.*). We no longer live after the flesh, but after the spirit.

The reason most Christians are scared of physical death is that they have so little experience with the spirit dimension. It's actually a fear of the unknown.

But when you get caught up in the Spirit and live in the Spirit with the greater Jesus, death loses its sting. It's no longer a big deal.

But, if you haven't so been "caught up," death still holds its sting for you. *"The sting of death is sin ..."* Adam was afraid of meeting God and he hid from Him (Genesis 3:10). Why? It's because he had sinned. The result of his sin was death. [Apostle] Paul said, *"For as in Adam all die, so in Christ all will be made alive"* (1 Corinthians 15:22). When we are dead in sin, all we know is the flesh.

The idea of losing that flesh is frightening, because we feel it is all there is of us. So we hang on to it. We try to make our flesh safe, secure, happy, and comfortable—because we think it's all we have.

But, when we are made alive spiritually and caught up in the air in Christ, we discover that our flesh is no longer our problem, or our treasure. We crucify it so we can be raised to even higher spiritually in Christ and in the power of the resurrection.

When that power takes over, the power of sin over us is gone. We can let the flesh go and live the resurrected life of Christ. We can walk supernaturally, unconsciously in the Spirit, now, in this life, and on this earth.

"The power of sin is the law ..." Many of us keep trying to earn immortality by doing things, by obeying the law. We've got this image from the Dark Ages of Saint Peter standing at the gates, weighing our good deeds against our bad deeds.

If getting into heaven through our good works of the flesh were possible, Christ's death on the cross would have been unnecessary.

New Testament reality is that the power of sin—the flesh's inability to fulfil the law—is broken by the fact of Christ's death and resurrection, and it is broken in us by our co-resurrection in Christ.

We are freed from doing the works of the flesh so that we can do the works of Jesus and even greater works by the power of his spirit. *"But thanks be to God! He gives us the victory through our Lord Jesus Christ."*

He gives—present tense—not will someday give. It is a great victory, here and now, not a great escape someday, by-and-by.

Please note, again, this major difference in human priorities and God's priorities.

Human beings think mostly in terms of surviving and staying physically healthy, prospering materially, being emotionally happy, and perhaps being morally good.

God's priorities are that we worship Him in spirit and truth, develop godly character (purity of heart), and that we reign and rule, spiritually and physically, with the greater Jesus in His Kingdom on this earth, here and now.

Oddly, enough, when we order our lives after God's priorities, we get more than we ever dreamed.

We don't just survive; we thrive; we don't just prosper materially; we gain the riches of Christ. We don't just have happiness, which can be destroyed by circumstances; we have his joy, which cannot be touched by circumstances—even by our own physical death, which will certainly happen someday (Hebrews 9:27).

At that time we shall enter Heaven, receive our new "spiritual body," and start enjoying our eternal rewards and/or suffering eternal loss.

In our next chapter, the final of this writing; we would be exploring another brief section adapted from Dr. John Noë's book "The Greater Jesus", which I have found to have some solid teaching on the resurrection. You can certainly read several of his books, which can be sourced at https://www.amazon.com/John-R.-Noe/e/B001K8QY7O

Chapter Six
UNDERSTANDING THE RESURRECTION OF THE DEAD ONES

[3]BODILY RESURRECTION OF THE DEAD ONES (PLURAL)
ALL THE PASSAGES USED BY POPULAR "RAPTURE" WRITERS AND TEACHERS WERE actually fulfilled by real and bodily resurrections.

What's more, they all occurred within the time frame Jesus specified (**"Assuredly, I say to you, this generation [which generation was being referred to here? Yes, of course <u>the generation Jesus was speaking to back in the 1st Century</u>] will by no means pass away till all these things take place."** [Emphasis and Parenthesis Author's] Matthew 24:34), and every New Testament writer and the 1st Century Church expected as they were guided into all truth by the Holy Spirit: John 16:13

However, when He, the Spirit of truth, has come, He will guide you into all truth; for He will not speak on His own authority, but whatever He hears He will speak; and He will tell you things to come.

Unfortunately, these occurrences are some of the most ignored, distorted, confused, and misunderstood realities and concepts in Christianity. No more! Key passages are: 1 Thessalonians 4:13-18 and 1 Corinthians 15.

---
[3] Adapted from Dr. John Noë's book "The Greater Jesus", sourced at https://www.amazon.com/John-R.-Noe/e/B001K8QY7O

But I do not want you to be ignorant, brethren, concerning those who have fallen asleep, lest you sorrow as others who have no hope. For if we believe that Jesus died and rose again, even so God will bring with Him those who sleep in Jesus. For this we say to you by the word of the Lord, that we who are alive and remain until the coming of the Lord will by no means precede those who are asleep. For the Lord Himself will descend from heaven with a shout, with the voice of an archangel, and with the trumpet of God. And the dead in Christ will rise first. Then we who are alive and remain shall be caught up together with them in the clouds to meet the Lord in the air. And thus we shall always be with the Lord. Therefore comfort one another with these words.

In the 1 Corinthians passage we find an ordering, or sequencing, for these resurrection occurrences is revealed:
1 Corinthians 15:20-24

*But now is Christ risen from the dead, and become the firstfruits of them that slept. For since by man came death, by man came also the resurrection of the dead. For as in Adam all die, even so in Christ shall all be made alive. But every man in his own **order**: Christ the firstfruits; afterward they that are Christ's at his coming. Then cometh the end, when he shall have delivered up the kingdom to God, even the Father; when he shall have put down all rule and all authority and power. (Emphasis Author's 1 Corinthians 15:20-24)*

*But Christ has indeed been raised from the dead, the firstfruits of those who have fallen asleep. For since death came through a man, the resurrection of the dead comes also through a man. For as in Adam all die, so in Christ all will be made alive. But each in his own **turn**: Christ, the firstfruits; then, when he comes, those who belong to him. Then the end will come, when he hands over the kingdom to God the Father after he has destroyed all dominion, authority and power. (Emphasis Author's NIV 1 Corinthians 15:20-24)*

The Greek word translated "turn" or "order" is tagma. This is the only place in the New Testament where it's used.

Tagma is a military term that means "a series or succession."

The thought is of soldiers marching or of a parade in which others follow along individually. This "ordering" beautifully harmonizes with what happened back then in the 1st Century and with all the other fulfilments that have occurred.

The author of the "Left Behind" series tell us, that for over nineteen centuries and counting these inspired words of *[Apostle]* Paul have not been fulfilled, then the non-occurrence of this event presents a highly problematic dilemma and I will outline why.

- The *[Apostle]* Paul's words of encouragement turned out to be a cruel misrepresentation in the lives of his original readers.
- 1st-Century Believers actually ended up deceiving each other with these words rather than encouraging each other with 1 Thessalonians 4:13, 18) ("*But I do not want you to be ignorant, brethren, concerning those who have fallen asleep, lest you sorrow as others who have no hope.* **Therefore comfort one another with these words**." (Emphasis Author's)

And they died "in vain" not having received what they expected in their lifetime. (1 Corinthians 15:14)

"And if Christ is not risen, then our preaching is empty and your faith is also empty." (Emphasis Author's)

- If *[Apostle]* Paul's Holy-Spirit-guided imminent expectations proved false, how can we trust him to have conveyed other aspects of the faith along to us correctly? Harken to these words in John 16:13

However, when He, the Spirit of truth, has come, He will guide you into all truth; for He will not speak on His own authority, but whatever He hears He will speak; and He will tell you things to come.

So now let's see if we can arrive at a better understanding, from a sola Scriptura standpoint, of the order and time of fulfillment in four successive resurrection stages.

STAGE #1—JESUS' RESURRECTION

The bodily resurrection of Jesus Christ is one of the most well-attested and well-known facts of human history.

No other event has such overwhelming weight of evidence and left such an impact on the world.

But even though Jesus' resurrection is basically uncontested in conservative evangelical circles, how and when an individual Believer participates in Christ's resurrection, here and now and upon physical death, has been one of the most distorted, confused, and misunderstood concepts in the Christian faith.

What is also not well-known is that this event marked the beginning of the "last days"/eschatological resurrection of the dead ones (plural). Why so?

It's because other resurrections "out of the graves" also occurred in that 1st Century. Therefore, Jesus' resurrection was not an isolated event separated by Centuries of time from a yet-future resurrection.

But He was the "*firstborn from the dead*" (Colossians 1:18 "*And He is the head of the body, the church, who is the beginning, the firstborn from the dead, that in all things He may have the pre-eminence.*")

He was also actually the "First" of the "*firstfruits*" (1 Corinthians 15:20-23 "*But now Christ is risen from the dead, and has become the firstfruits of those who have fallen asleep. For since by man came death, by Man also came the resurrection of the dead. For as in Adam all die, even so in Christ all shall be made alive.* **But each one in his own order**: *Christ the firstfruits, afterward those who are Christ's at His coming.*") Emphasis added

STAGE #2—MORE BODILY RESURRECTIONS

Using harvest imagery and the metaphor of the "*firstfruits*," more resurrections took place as the bodies of many (not all) Old Testament Saints came out of their graves and paraded through the streets of Jerusalem: Matthew 27:51-53

> *And behold, the veil of the temple was torn in two from top to bottom, and the earth shook; and the rocks split, and the tombs were opened; and* **many bodies of the saints who had fallen asleep were raised**; *and coming out of the tombs (graves), and after his*

[Jesus'] resurrection they entered the holy city [Jerusalem] and appeared to many. Emphasis and Parenthesis Author's

Obviously, some kind of literal and bodily (soma) resurrection took place after Jesus' death and resurrection.

Not surprisingly, many interpreters have tried to sidestep, downplay, or ignore this biblically recorded and collective event.

But this one thing is for sure.

This event confirms that they were living in the eschatological and biblical "*last days*," back then and there, because the general resurrection of the dead was now underway. Let's look at the following passages:

Daniel 12

At that time Michael shall stand up, The great prince who stands watch over the sons of your people; And there shall be a time of trouble, Such as never was since there was a nation, Even to that time. And at that time your people shall be delivered, Every one who is found written in the book. **<u>And many of those who sleep in the dust of the earth shall awake, Some to everlasting life, Some to shame and everlasting contempt</u>**. *Those who are wise shall shine Like the brightness of the firmament, And those who turn many to righteousness Like the stars forever and ever.* "**But you, Daniel, shut up the words, and seal the book until the time of the end**; *many shall run to and fro, and knowledge shall increase.*" *Then I, Daniel, looked; and there stood two others, one on this riverbank and the other on that riverbank. And one said to the man clothed in linen, who was above the waters of the river, "How long shall the fulfillment of these wonders be?" Then I heard the man clothed in linen, who was above the waters of the river, when he held up his right hand and his left hand to heaven, and swore by Him who lives forever, that it shall be for a time, times, and half a time; and* **when the power of the holy people has been completely shattered, all these things shall be finished**. *Although I heard, I did not understand. Then I said, "My lord, what shall be the end of these things?" And he said, "Go your way, Daniel,* **for the words are closed up and sealed till the time of the end** [<u>what end is being referred to here?</u>]. *Many* shall be purified, made white, and refined, but the wicked shall do wickedly; and none of the wicked shall understand, but the wise shall understand. "And from the time that the daily sacrifice is taken away, and the abomination of desolation is set up, there shall be one thousand two hundred and ninety days. Blessed is he who waits, and comes to the one thousand three hundred and thirty-five days. **"But you, go your way till the end; for you shall rest, and will arise to your inheritance at the end of the days**." (Emphasis and Parenthesis Author's)

John 5:28-29

Do not marvel at this; for the hour is coming in which all who are in the graves will hear His voice and come forth—those who have done good, to the resurrection of life, and those who have done evil, to the resurrection of condemnation.

No doubt, this was why the *[Apostle]* Paul, during his defense before King Agrippa remarked, *"Why should any of you consider it incredible that God raises the dead?"* (Acts 26:8).

The Greek word translated "dead" here is actually in the plural, i.e., "dead ones" or "dead persons." [*It is the word:* νεκρῶν οἱ *μὲν translated –* dead ones].

This is the proper translation. For more plural usages see:
Acts 17:32

And when they heard of the resurrection of the dead, some mocked, while others said, "We will hear you again on this matter.

Acts 23:6

But when Paul perceived that one part were Sadducees and the other Pharisees, he cried out in the council, "Men and brethren, I am a Pharisee, the son of a Pharisee; concerning the hope and resurrection of the dead I am being judged!

Acts 24:21

unless it is for this one statement which I cried out, standing among them, 'Concerning the resurrection of the dead I am being judged by you this day.'

Acts 26:23

that the Christ would suffer, that He would be the first to rise from the dead, and would proclaim light to the Jewish people and to the Gentiles.

1 Corinthians 15:12-16

Now if Christ is preached that He has been raised from the dead, how do some among you say that there is no resurrection of the dead? But if there is no resurrection of the dead, then Christ is not risen. And if Christ is not risen, then our preaching is empty and your faith is also empty. Yes, and we are found false witnesses of God, because we have testified of God that He raised up Christ, whom He did not raise up—if in fact the dead do not rise. For if the dead do not rise, then Christ is not risen.

But resurrection for the rest of the dead ones (the harvest) was still being anticipated as the New Testament was being penned.

STAGE #3—RESURRECTION DAY FOR THE REST OF THE DEAD ONES

Thirty years after the above two resurrection events, the *[Apostle]* Paul wrote when he was accused of sedition and brought before Felix to plead his case:

Acts 24:14-15

*But this I confess to you, that according to the Way which they call a sect, so I worship the God of my fathers, believing all things which are written in the Law and in the Prophets. I have hope in God, which they themselves also accept, that there will be **[to be about***

***to be]** a resurrection of the dead, both of the just [righteous] and the unjust [wicked]."* (Emphasis and Parenthesis Author's)

Two of *[Apostle]* Paul's key words in this passage are mellein esesthai.
Traditionally, they have been translated as "will be" or "shall be." In the literal Greek, however, they are: "**to be about to be**."

This double-intensified force of imminent occurrence is missed in nearly all the major English translations of the Bible.

But the dye was already cast.

The resurrection harvest had already begun. All that awaited was the "**last day**"—singular: of the "last days"—plural…

John 6:39-40

*This is the will of the Father who sent Me, that of all He has given Me I should lose nothing, but should raise it up at **the last day**. And this is the will of Him who sent Me, that everyone who sees the Son and believes in Him may have everlasting life; and I will raise him up at **the last day**.* (Emphasis Author's)

John 6:44

*No one can come to Me unless the Father who sent Me draws him; and I will raise him up at **the last day**.* (Emphasis Author's)

John 6:54

*Whoever eats My flesh and drinks My blood has eternal life, and I will raise him up at **the last day**.* (Emphasis Author's)

John 11:24

*Martha said to Him, "I know that he will rise again in the resurrection at **the last day**."* (Emphasis Author's)

Of the "**last days**" —plural:

Hebrews 1:2

God, who at various times and in various ways spoke in time past to the fathers by the prophets, has in **these last days spoken to us by His Son***, whom He has appointed heir of all things, through whom also He made the worlds;* (Emphasis Author's)

And again "**the harvest is the end of the age**" Matthew 13:36-39

Then Jesus sent the multitude away and went into the house. And His disciples came to Him, saying, "Explain to us the parable of the tares of the field." He answered and said to them: "He who sows the good seed is the Son of Man. The field is the world, the good seeds are the sons of the kingdom, but the tares are the sons of the wicked one. The enemy who sowed them is the devil, **the harvest is the end of the age***, [***which age is Jesus referring to here***?] and the reapers are the angels.* (Emphasis and Paraphrase Author's)

He Was Speaking Of The Jewish/Old Covenant Age And Not The End Of Time… Matthew 24:3, 34

Now as He sat on the Mount of Olives, the disciples came to Him privately, saying, "Tell us, when will these things be? And what will be the sign of Your coming, and of **the end of the age***?" … "Assuredly, I say to you, this generation [***which generation was Jesus referring to? His generation***!] will by no means pass away till all these things take place."* (Emphasis and Paraphrase Author's)

And that was in fulfillment of Daniel 12:4,7

"But you, Daniel, shut up the words, and seal the book until the time of the end **[*what end is being referred to here? The end of the Old Covenant, the end of the Jewish Age*]***; many shall run to and fro, and knowledge shall increase." … "Then I heard the man clothed in linen, who was above the waters of the river, when he held up his right hand and his left hand to heaven, and swore by Him who lives forever, that it shall be for a time, times, and half a*

time; and when the power of the holy people has been completely shattered, all these things shall be finished." (Emphasis and Paraphrase Author's)

Please note that the Christian Age (the age to come, the Kingdom Age, the Messianic Age, and even for the world) has no end and, therefore, no "last day" upon which to place a resurrection of this harvest. Let us look at the following passages to confirm this:

Isaiah 9:6-7

For unto us a Child is born, Unto us a Son is given; And the government will be upon His shoulder. And His name will be called Wonderful, Counsellor, Mighty God, Everlasting Father, Prince of Peace. Of the increase of His government and peace There will be no end, Upon the throne of David and over His kingdom, To order it and establish it with judgment and justice From that time forward, even forever. The zeal of the Lord of hosts will perform this.

Daniel 2:44

And in the days of these kings the God of heaven will set up a kingdom which shall never be destroyed; and the kingdom shall not be left to other people; it shall break in pieces and consume all these kingdoms, and it shall stand forever.

Daniel 7:13-14

I was watching in the night visions, And behold, One like the Son of Man, Coming with the clouds of heaven! He came to the Ancient of Days, And they brought Him near before Him. Then to Him was given dominion and glory and a kingdom, That all peoples, nations, and languages should serve Him. His dominion is an everlasting dominion, Which shall not pass away, And His kingdom the one Which shall not be destroyed.

Luke 1:32-35

He will be great, and will be called the Son of the Highest; and the Lord God will give Him the throne of His father David. And He will reign over the house of Jacob forever, and of His kingdom there will be no end." Then Mary said to the angel, "How can this be, since I do not know a man?" And the angel answered and said to her, "The Holy Spirit will come upon you, and the power of the Highest will overshadow you; therefore, also, that Holy One who is to be born will be called the Son of God."

Ephesians 3:20-21

Now to Him who is able to do exceedingly abundantly above all that we ask or think, according to the power that works in us, to Him be glory in the church by Christ Jesus to all generations, forever and ever. Amen.

Hebrews 12:28

Therefore, since we are receiving a kingdom which cannot be shaken, let us have grace, by which we may serve God acceptably with reverence and godly fear.

So, what else is there in Scripture or logic to justify postponing this resurrection of the rest of the dead ones from Hades?

That day came! At some point in the late summer or early fall of A.D. 70, or perhaps two or three years later in A.D. 72 or 73—when **the last stone was removed**:

Matthew 24:2

And Jesus said to them, "Do you not see all these things? Assuredly, I say to you, not one stone shall be left here upon another, that shall not be thrown down."

THE FIELD PLOUGHED OVER
Micah 3:12

> *Therefore because of you Zion shall be ploughed like a field, Jerusalem shall become heaps of ruins, And the mountain of the temple Like the bare hills of the forest.*

Jeremiah 26:17-18

> *Then certain of the elders of the land rose up and spoke to all the assembly of the people, saying: "Micah of Moresheth prophesied in the days of Hezekiah king of Judah, and spoke to all the people of Judah, saying, 'Thus says the L*ORD *of hosts: "Zion shall be ploughed like a field, Jerusalem shall become heaps of ruins, And the mountain of the temple Like the bare hills of the forest."'*

AND THE PROPHESIED POINT OF "DESOLATION" REACHED
Matthew 23:37-38

> *O Jerusalem, Jerusalem, the one who kills the prophets and stones those who are sent to her! How often I wanted to gather your children together, as a hen gathers her chicks under her wings, but you were not willing! See! Your house is left to you desolate…*

But unlike before, and in keeping with the applied harvest metaphor, no resurrection bodies were seen rising out of graves or parading around Jerusalem.

Rather, their souls were taken out of the hadean realm, that spirit-realm holding place of the dead, taken to heaven (bypassing earth), and given their judgment and "spiritual" resurrection bodies (1 Corinthians 15:44). This end is history.

It all took place within the spirit realm and within the time span of Jesus' "this generation" (Matthew 24:34).

Moreover, this fulfillment is in perfect harmony with the immanency expectations of every New Testament writer and the early Christian community (John 16:13 *However, when He, the Spirit of truth, has come,*

He will guide you into all truth; for He will not speak on His own authority, but whatever He hears He will speak; and He will tell you things to come.).

This often prophesied and imminently expected end was covenantal, and not cosmic. Once again, it occurred within history, and not at history's end—for which there is no end and, therefore, no "last day" upon which to have a resurrection.

STAGE #4—POST END (TELOS)—THE ONGOING REALITY—"EACH" OR "EVERY MAN IN HIS OWN TURN/ORDER."

From that time of the end of the age on, the next Saint to physically die, never again went to Hades, that temporary, spirit-realm holding place of the dead, to await resurrection and judgment.

Please understand this: Jesus, who holds "*the keys to death and Hades*" (Revelation 1:18; 20:13-14) had emptied it out and locked it up, forever.

Therefore, after Resurrection Day on the "last day," it's straight to heaven upon physical death for Believers to receive their judgment and a new, "spiritual body" (1 Corinthians 15:44), which God "gives" (1 Corinthians 15:38). Heaven's door is now open wide.

This fulfilled reality is in contrast to no one being in Heaven prior to, during, and for some time after Jesus' earthly ministry (see John 3:13 *No one has ascended to heaven but He who came down from heaven, that is, the Son of Man who is in heaven.*; 13:33 *Little children, I shall be with you a little while longer. You will seek Me; and as I said to the Jews, 'Where I am going, you cannot come,' so now I say to you.*, 36 *Simon Peter said to Him, "Lord, where are You going?" Jesus answered him, "Where I am going you cannot follow Me now, but you shall follow Me afterward."*). Thus, the "*last enemy*" of "*death*" was destroyed (1 Corinthians 15:26) and "*swallowed up in victory*" (1 Corinthians 15:54; Isaiah 25:8). That last enemy was not death itself.

Living and dying still continue and always will (Hebrews 9:27). What was terminated was the temporary holding place of the dead, Hades or Sheol. No more would it prevail (Matthew 16:18 *And I also say to you that you are Peter, and on this rock I will build My church, and the gates of Hades shall not prevail against it.*).

Yes, this end-time fulfillment has been largely misunderstood, ignored, and/or denied, to our detriment.

From then on, it's only one step from this life to the judgment and resurrection state in heaven. Thus, Revelation's proclamation, "*Blessed are the dead who die in the Lord from now on*" (Revelation 14:13) has been fulfilled.

It's all a done deal and part of "*the faith that was once for all delivered to the saints*" (Jude 3)! "*Therefore, encourage each other with these words*" (1 Thessalonians 4:18).

'BONES-ARE-STILL-IN-THE-GRAVES' OBJECTION.

Critical Objection: Not so, insist the vast majority of Christian scholars. Go to any graveyard, dig up a grave, they insist, and we can prove that this "last day" resurrection has not yet taken place. Why not? It's because the "bones are still in the graves." And one day, "at the end of this present age, God will reunite our souls with our bodies."

This objection is simply a misunderstanding of the nature of bodily resurrection. It's assumed that since Jesus' self-same earthly and physical body arose from the grave, so will our old dead, decayed, and perhaps decomposed bodies. But is this assumption biblically accurate?

Here are three reasons why it is not:

1. Jesus' Body was the only one promised not to see decay (Acts 2:25-27 *For David says concerning Him: 'I foresaw the LORD always before my face, For He is at my right hand, that I may not be shaken. Therefore my heart rejoiced, and my tongue was glad; Moreover my flesh also will rest in hope. For You will not leave my soul in Hades, Nor will You allow Your Holy One to see corruption.*, Acts 2:31-32 *he, foreseeing this, spoke concerning the resurrection of the Christ, that His soul was not left in Hades, nor did His flesh see corruption. This Jesus God has raised up, of which we are all witnesses.* Acts 13:33-35 *God has fulfilled this for us their children, in that He has raised up Jesus. As it is also written in the second Psalm: 'You are My Son, Today I have begotten You.' And that He raised Him from the dead, no more to return to corruption, He has spoken thus: 'I will give you the sure mercies of David.' Therefore He also says in another Psalm: 'You will not allow Your Holy One to see corruption.'* from Psalms 16:10 *For You will not leave my soul in Sheol, Nor will You allow Your Holy One to see corruption.*; 49:9 *That he should continue to live eternally, And not see the Pit.*).

2. This promise was made only to the Messiah and to no one else. The rest of us are told *"for dust you are and to dust you will return"* (Genesis 2:7; 3:19; 1 Kings 2:1-2; Psalms 90:3).

And the L*ord* *God formed man of the dust of the ground, and breathed into his nostrils the breath of life; and man became a living being.*

In the sweat of your face you shall eat bread Till you return to the ground, For out of it you were taken; For dust you are, And to dust you shall return.

Now the days of David drew near that he should die, and he charged Solomon his son, saying: "I go the way of all the earth; be strong, therefore, and prove yourself a man."

3. God does not need our old and perhaps scattered atoms and molecules from our previous physical body to give us a new "spiritual body" (1 Corinthians 15:35-38, 44).

But someone will say, "How are the dead raised up? And with what body do they come?" Foolish one, what you sow is not made alive unless it dies. And what you sow, you do not sow that body that shall be, but mere grain—perhaps wheat or some other grain. But God gives it a body as He pleases, and to each seed its own body... It is sown a natural body, it is raised a spiritual body. There is a natural body, and there is a spiritual body.

In *[Apostle]* Paul's seed analogy in 1 Corinthians 15:37, the outer shell of a seed is left behind, stays in the ground, and decomposes. It does not become part of the new plant.

The seed holds the germ of the new body, which is something greater. So, our physical earthly body holds the germ (the Spirit of the Godhead) of something greater (the "spiritual body").

What could be any clearer than this? Scripture never speaks of us receiving a resurrected and rejuvenated, old, decayed, decomposed, earthly, and physical body.

In accordance with *[Apostle]* Paul's seed analogy, we shed that shell at death. Such a big difference!

Consequently, the Bible never mentions a "**resurrection of the body**," "**resurrection of the flesh**," "**resurrected body**," or "**physical resurrection**."

Instead, the Bible uses two inspired phrases: "**_the resurrection of the dead_**" and "**dead ones**" Let us look at the following passages: Matthew 22:31-32

> *But concerning **the resurrection of the dead**, have you not read what was spoken to you by God, saying, 'I am the God of Abraham, the God of Isaac, and the God of Jacob'? God is not the God of the dead, but of the living. And when the multitudes heard this, they were astonished at His teaching.* (Emphasis Author's)

Acts 17:32

> *And when they heard of **the resurrection of the dead**, some mocked, while others said, "We will hear you again on this matter.* (Emphasis Author's)

Acts 23:6

> *But when Paul perceived that one part were Sadducees and the other Pharisees, he cried out in the council, "Men and brethren, I am a Pharisee, the son of a Pharisee; concerning the hope and **resurrection of the dead** I am being judged!"* (Emphasis Author's)

Acts 24:15

> *I have hope in God, which they themselves also accept, that there will be a **resurrection of the dead**, both of the just and the unjust.* (Emphasis Author's)

Acts 24:21

*unless it is for this one statement which I cried out, standing among them, 'Concerning **the resurrection of the dead** I am being judged by you this day.' (Emphasis Author's)*

1 Corinthians 15:12-13

*Now if Christ is preached that He has been raised from the dead, how do some among you say that there is no **resurrection of the dead**? But if there is no **resurrection of the dead**, then Christ is not risen. (Emphasis Author's)*

1 Corinthians 15:21

*For since by man came death, by Man also came **the resurrection of the dead**. (Emphasis Author's)*

1 Corinthians 15:42

*So also is **the resurrection of the dead**. The body is sown in corruption, it is raised in incorruption. (Emphasis Author's)*

Hebrews 6:1-2

*Therefore, leaving the discussion of the elementary principles of Christ, let us go on to perfection, not laying again the foundation of repentance from dead works and of faith toward God, of the doctrine of baptisms, of laying on of hands, of **resurrection of the dead**, and of eternal judgment. (Emphasis Author's)*

And "**resurrection from the dead**" Let us likewise look at these passages:

Luke 20:35

But those who are counted worthy to attain that age, and **the resurrection from the dead***, neither marry nor are given in marriage...* (Emphasis Author's)

Acts 4:1-2

Now as they spoke to the people, the priests, the captain of the temple, and the Sadducees came upon them, being greatly disturbed that they taught the people and preached in Jesus **the resurrection from the dead***.* (Emphasis Author's)

Romans 1:3-4

concerning His Son Jesus Christ our Lord, who was born of the seed of David according to the flesh, and declared to be the Son of God with power according to the Spirit of holiness, by **the resurrection from the dead***.* (Emphasis Author's)

Philippians 3:10-11

that I may know Him and the power of His resurrection, and the fellowship of His sufferings, being conformed to His death, if, by any means, I may attain to **the resurrection from the dead***.* (Emphasis Author's)

AGAIN, BIG DIFFERENCE!

And remember this: flesh and blood will not inherit the Kingdom. Here is what the *[Apostle]* Paul said in 1 Corinthians 15:50:

Now this I say, brethren, that <u>*flesh and blood cannot inherit the kingdom of God*</u>*; nor does corruption inherit incorruption.* (Emphasis Author's)

So, what will our new "spiritual body" be like? All we are told is, it *"will be like his [Jesus'] glorious body"* (Philippians 3:21).

Consequently, this resurrection body may be both material and immaterial, physical and spirit.

I like what two writers Ken Boa and Robert Bowman Jr. have stated succinctly, "the Bible offers no formal definition of 'death' and no detailed exposition of what happens to people when they die."

Therefore, they further explain, "we must infer our understanding of death [and resurrection] from a whole range of biblical statements pertaining to the subject." But one other thing is also for sure. None of these resurrection verses promised a future rapture-removal of a group of living, breathing Believers and dead corpses off the surface of planet Earth.

As we have seen, resurrection reality continues after death when we receive our new "spiritual body" that God gives (1 Corinthians 15:38, 44), and there is more.

Truly, truly, and here and now, the Christian life is a "high calling" (Philippians 3:14 *I press toward the goal for the prize of the upward call of God in Christ Jesus.*; 2 Thessalonians 1:11 *Therefore we also pray always for you that our God would count you worthy of this calling, and fulfill all the good pleasure of His goodness and the work of faith with power,*; Hebrews 3:1 *Therefore, holy brethren, partakers of the heavenly calling, consider the Apostle and High Priest of our confession, Christ Jesus,*; 2 Peter 1:10 *Therefore, brethren, be even more diligent to make your call and election sure, for if you do these things you will never stumble;*; Ephesians 4:1, 4 *I, therefore, the prisoner of the Lord, beseech you to walk worthy of the calling with which you were called, There is one body and one Spirit, just as you were called in one hope of your calling;*) and an example to be set (Titus 2:7 *in all things showing yourself to be a pattern of good works; in doctrine showing integrity, reverence, incorruptibility,*).

To "walk as Jesus did" requires unwavering belief, total trust, and a yielded spirit.

It produces godly character that results in proper conduct glorifying to God. Such a life is realizable on this earth and in this human body.

Jesus did it! [Apostle] Paul did it.

They are our models of the Christian life in (1 Corinthians 11:1 *Imitate me, just as I also imitate Christ.*; 2 Corinthians 10:3-6 *For though we walk in the flesh, we do not war according to the flesh. For the weapons of our warfare are not carnal but mighty in God for pulling down strongholds, casting down arguments and every high thing that exalts itself against the knowledge of God, bringing every thought into captivity to the obedience of Christ, and being ready to punish all disobedience when your obedience is fulfilled.*), as well as among the Thessalonians (1 Thessalonians 1:4-9 *knowing, beloved brethren, your election by God. For our gospel did not come to you in word only, but also in power, and in the Holy Spirit and in much assurance, as you know what kind of men we were among you for your sake. And you became followers of us and of the Lord, having received the word in much affliction, with joy of the Holy Spirit, so that you became examples to all in Macedonia and Achaia who believe. For from you the word of the Lord has sounded forth, not only in Macedonia and Achaia, but also in every place. Your faith toward God has gone out, so that we do not need to say anything. For they themselves declare concerning us what manner of entry we had to you, and how you turned to God from idols to serve the living and true God,*). Dare we make any less of it as so many have? [End of quote]

When Jesus Christ was manifested in the flesh, He came as Saviour to die for the sins of the world. At that time the Jews completely missed why He was there and they wanted Him to set up His Kingdom with them and to overthrow the Roman Empire/rule. He rejected that idea as He was on a mission to die for the sins of the world. However, after His death, burial and resurrection, He rose triumphantly as King of His Kingdom to reign forever in both Heaven and on earth.

Here is what I believe the Scriptures teach us: flesh and blood cannot enter the Kingdom of Heaven so that when a Believer dies his or her flesh must put on immortality to enter the Heavenly realm. As Believers we do not have to wait for some future date to be in the Presence of the Lord when we die. There is no holding place. When we die, we go directly and immediately into the Presence of the Lord as a Born-Again Believer in Jesus Christ.

There is so much more that can be said about the Resurrection, that it will take many, many more books to completely deal with this all-important pillar of the Christian Faith. However, I would like to leave you with the following all-important passage from one of *[Apostle]* Paul's letters to the Corinthian church concerning the Resurrection:

Chapter Six: Understanding the Resurrection of the Dead Ones

1 Corinthians 15:12-58

But if it is preached that Christ has been raised from the dead, how can some of you say that there is no resurrection of the dead? If there is no resurrection of the dead, then not even Christ has been raised. And if Christ has not been raised, our preaching is useless and so is your faith. More than that, we are then found to be false witnesses about God, for we have testified about God that he raised Christ from the dead. But he did not raise him if in fact the dead are not raised. For if the dead are not raised, then Christ has not been raised either. And if Christ has not been raised, your faith is futile; you are still in your sins. Then those also who have fallen asleep in Christ are lost. If only for this life we have hope in Christ, we are to be pitied more than all men. But Christ has indeed been raised from the dead, the first-fruits of those who have fallen asleep. For since death came through a man, the resurrection of the dead comes also through a man. For as in Adam all die, so in Christ all will be made alive. But each in his own turn: Christ, the first-fruits; then, when he comes, those who belong to him. Then the end will come, when he hands over the kingdom to God the Father after he has destroyed all dominion, authority and power. For he must reign until he has put all his enemies under his feet. The last enemy to be destroyed is death. For he "has put everything under his feet." Now when it says that "everything" has been put under him, it is clear that this does not include God himself, who put everything under Christ. When he has done this, then the Son himself will be made subject to him who put everything under him, so that God may be all in all. Now if there is no resurrection, what will those do who are baptized for the dead? If the dead are not raised at all, why are people baptized for them? And as for us, why do we endanger ourselves every hour? I die every day—I mean that, brothers—just as surely as I glory over you in Christ Jesus our Lord. If I fought wild beasts in Ephesus for merely human reasons, what have I gained? If the dead are not raised, "Let us eat and drink, for tomorrow we die." Do not be misled: "Bad company corrupts good character." Come back to your senses as you ought, and stop sinning; for there are some who are ignorant of God—I say this to your shame. But someone may ask,

"**How are the dead raised? With what kind of body will they come?**" How foolish! What you sow does not come to life unless it dies. **When you sow, you do not plant the body that will be, but just a seed, perhaps of wheat or of something else. But God gives it a body as he has determined**, and to each kind of seed he gives its own body. All flesh is not the same: Men have one kind of flesh, animals have another, birds another and fish another. There are also heavenly bodies and there are earthly bodies; but the splendour of the heavenly bodies is one kind, and the splendour of the earthly bodies is another. The sun has one kind of splendour, the moon another and the stars another; and star differs from star in splendour. So will it be with the resurrection of the dead. The body that is sown is perishable, it is raised imperishable; it is sown in dishonour, it is raised in glory; it is sown in weakness, it is raised in power; it is sown a natural body, it is raised a spiritual body. If there is a natural body, there is also a spiritual body. So it is written: "The first man Adam became a living being"; the last Adam, a life-giving spirit. The spiritual did not come first, but the natural, and after that the spiritual. The first man was of the dust of the earth, the second man from heaven. As was the earthly man, so are those who are of the earth; and as is the man from heaven, so also are those who are of heaven. And just as we have borne the likeness of the earthly man, so shall we bear the likeness of the man from heaven. I declare to you, brothers, that flesh and blood cannot inherit the kingdom of God, nor does the perishable inherit the imperishable. Listen, I tell you a mystery: We will not all sleep, but we will all be changed—in a flash, in the twinkling of an eye, **at the last trumpet. For the trumpet will sound, the dead will be raised imperishable, and we will be changed.** For the perishable must clothe itself with the imperishable, and the mortal with immortality. When the perishable has been clothed with the imperishable, and the mortal with immortality, then the saying that is written will come true: "Death has been swallowed up in victory." "Where, O death, is your victory? Where, O death, is your sting?" The sting of death is sin, and the power of sin is the law. But thanks be to God! He gives us the victory through our Lord Jesus Christ. Therefore, my dear brothers, stand firm. Let nothing move you. Always give yourselves fully to the work *of the Lord, because you know that your labour in the Lord is not in vain. Emphasis Author's*

It is my earnest prayer that truth contained within the pages of this book will accomplish a few things. I trust that it will start the spiritual conversation as to what really happens after death and resurrection for the believer in Christ. I hope that many will come to see the powerful application of understanding the Scriptures from a 1st Century mindset and also understanding "audience relevance." And lastly, that we who are now living in the 21st Century must have a better understanding of Scripture if we are to successfully navigate the spiritual terrain before us. Shalom!

Other Exciting Titles
BY MICHAEL SCANTLEBURY

NAVIGATING THROUGH SPIRITUAL TRANSITIONS
We are all in transition. It's a natural phase of life for us. Transitions can take many forms, as I am sure you've experienced yourself.

Transitions build stories and reveal the history of our lives. They happen whether you desire them to or not. There is no way around them unless you are dead. So, if you are choosing life, anticipate and prepare for transitions. They are coming and will come again.

According to the dictionary, a "transition" is **a Movement, Passage, or Change from One Position to Another.** The word "transition" is often used in human services to refer to the general process of someone moving, or being moved, from one set of services or circumstances to another.

As Christians, each transition period we go through, God is leading us to ensure that we come into the fullness of all that He has promised in and through our local houses/churches. This leading He does with the many local houses/churches across the earth that are also experiencing various transition periods! However, I believe that there are dangers to be aware of in this journey as we stride towards our destiny.

Every leader regardless of his or her calling in life will experience seasons of transition. We make the common assumption that once we've arrived at a certain place that we are beyond being tested. It is not so!

Those who serve closest to a leader when in transition must know how to stick in both good and bad times. Times of certainty and times of uncertainty.

It is my earnest prayer that this book will aide you in your times of transition!

EXPLORING THE SECRETS OF HIDDEN WEALTH

This masterpiece, has been quite controversial in some quarters, the subject of finances in the Kingdom. In his usual straight forward but yet biblical approach, Apostle diligently explained the parables of Jesus in view of provisions, delving into a strong theological framework for stewardship and how to form relevant partnership for wealth which is an effective interaction with the world system for material advance and contentment as a Kingdom virtue.

This book served to fuel in us an even deeper personal search into God's intention for wealth among His people. It provides a unique perspective on God's heart towards us and His empowering ability, through resources, to bring His purpose to pass.

"Exploring the Secrets of Hidden Wealth" is a revelatory guide to understanding the power, purpose and stewardship of money.

GOD'S ETERNAL PLAN

Let me quote this very important passage of Scripture: Hebrews 11:1-3

> *Now faith is the substance of things hoped for, the evidence of things not seen. For by it the elders obtained a good testimony. By faith we understand that the worlds were framed by the word of God, so that the things which are seen were not made of things which are visible.*

So, this is the premise from which this book would be written. We cannot even begin to understand the Scriptures or the heart of God if we do not believe that He is. And to do that we must enact the faith that everyone of us were given at birth according to: Romans 12:3

Because God always existed, we must understand and believe that He existed outside of space and time in the realm called *Eternal*. I believe that this is why we could understand the following passage of Scripture: Matthew 25:34-40

So, He knew exactly what He was seeking to accomplish, and nothing could take Him by surprise.

And that *time,* as we know it only began when He created it. This was done when He created the Heavens and the earth as recorded in the book of Genesis, when He established the sun and the moon and day and night causing, the establishment of days and night, and the record of days.

UNDERSTANDING THE DUAL ASPECTS OF FAITH

From the onset, Apostle Scantlebury presents the tenets of his tome, by eloquently contrasting the two dimensions of Faith: (1) where we use our Faith to acquire and believe God for new things and victories in Him and (2) where we use that same Faith to resist and battle against all odds that is thrown at us.

After defining the elements of faith, Apostle Michael empowers us with the tools to increase our faith: Our knowledge of God and the application of what we know. It's not enough to know what the Word of God says. What produces real faith is displayed when our actions match our belief.

Apostle Scantlebury gives us an accurate understanding of the benefits of our trials. Contrary to our Westernized belief, Faith and trials are mutually inclusive. We are encouraged to keep trusting God despite the opposition. Trusting God then becomes the substratum of having a pleasant relationship with Him.

UNDERSTANDING THE REVELATION

As we embark on this study, there are certain things that we need to first establish. Here are five things that I believe the book of Revelation is about:

1. Revelation is the most Biblical book in the Bible.
2. Revelation has a system of symbolism.
3. Revelation is a prophecy about imminent events – events that were about to break loose on the world of the First Century.
4. Revelation is a worship service.
5. Revelation is a book about dominion.

Also, we have to study The Revelation as a part of the entirety of Scripture and not as a separate book on its own. It ties in beautifully with the rest of the Bible and Israel's journey. So, as we study the prophecy within this book, we will see how it ties in with Jesus' prophecy recorded in Matthew 24 and many of the words spoken directly to the tribes of Israel. It was a powerful and very relevant book for the First Century Church and gives us today a clear picture of God's way of dealing with His people. When approached from this point of view, fresh realms of understanding will herald some fresh and powerful truths for us today.

Also, we need to bear in mind that the Bible is a record of Two Covenants; the Old Covenant which had a shelf life and was destined to come to an end. And then we have the New Covenant which is eternal and as such will never end. It has been eternally established by our King and Lord, Jesus the Christ. We need to add to this the understanding that the entire cannon of Scripture was written prior to AD 70.

ARE WE LIVING IN THE END TIMES OR THE LAST DAYS?

Whenever we hear this term "end-times or last-days" it conjures up all kinds of images in our minds: from the universe blowing up with the largest flames you could ever imagine! And that it would usher in a new heaven and a new earth. We also have presupposed in the body of Christ that before all of this would indeed occur, the righteous would be raptured away and then the world would be left a massive fire of destruction.

When you hear Christians mention the 'last days,' many just assume it's referring to the end of time and of the world. But the attentive Bible student asks, 'last days of what?' It seems obvious to me that the text is referring to the end of the Old Covenant-Temple aeon/age. When you read the New Testament through these lenses, all I can say is WOW! It makes a significant difference, when you read the Scriptures with the realization that the Bible was written FOR you and not TO you.

We need to also understand that "time of the end" and "end of time" are not one and the same thing. The Bible teaches about the "time of the end" but there is nothing taught about an "end of time."

FATHERS AND SONS – AN UNVEILING

As we embark upon this study, there is something that I would like for us to first understand, and it is this: God the Father is the ultimate Father. There has never been anyone like Him, nor is there currently anyone like Him, nor will there ever be anyone like Him. He is in a class all by Himself.

Another thing that we need to understand moving forward is this: Respect produced by force and domination is not respect but fear.

Also, when we speak of sons, we are not only referring to the male gender, but we are speaking of **a new class in God**. Those that have been washed by the Blood of Jesus and have entered the New Covenant with Him. Notice that in the Scriptures, it never states "Sons and Daughters of God."

John 1:12 states

But as many as received him, he gave them power to be made the sons of God, to them that believe in his name. ...

As such, I do believe that women can also be Apostles and in a broader scope, they qualify to "father" should that mantle be upon them.

HEAVEN & EARTH A BIBLICAL UNDERSTANDING
Whenever we today in this 21st Century read about heaven and earth in the Scriptures we need to be careful as to exactly what is being referred to. And here are some reasons as to why this must be.

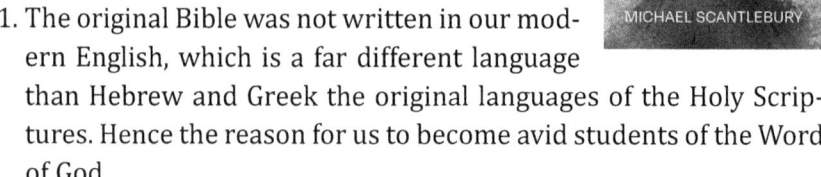

1. The original Bible was not written in our modern English, which is a far different language than Hebrew and Greek the original languages of the Holy Scriptures. Hence the reason for us to become avid students of the Word of God.
2. We, living today are not the original recipients of Scripture and as such we need to understand what the original recipients understood when they first received that Word.
3. We must be willing to let the Bible interpret itself and not hang on to our theories for the Scriptures.
4. That the Bible speaks of at least four Heavens and three earths. And as such we need to dig deep into the Word of God and find them and apply this understanding in our study.

Remember what the Scriptures say in Proverbs 25:2 *It is the glory of God to conceal the word, and the glory of kings to search out the speech.*

With that said let us now take a deeper dive and journey into the Word of God with the intention of extracting much needed revelation concerning these Heavens and Earths.

MY PONDERINGS

In this book before you the author has been engaged in pondering several subjects and as such, decided to put his thoughts in a book. As you read through these pages may the Lord use his thoughts to both inspire and bless you. Here are some of the subjects he has been pondering, with each one making up a chapter of this book:

My Ponderings on The Kingdom of God
My Ponderings on The Church
My Ponderings on Innovation
My Ponderings on Wisdom and The Power of Vision
My Ponderings on Navigating Seasons
My Ponderings on Breakthroughs
My Ponderings on Unity
My Ponderings on The Many Comings of Jesus
My Ponderings on Eschatology
My Ponderings on Jesus the First Fruit of the Dead
My Ponderings on Understanding the Times
My Ponderings on Understanding the New Covenant
My Ponderings on Gold

UNDERSTANDING THE KINGDOM OF GOD AND THE CHURCH OF JESUS CHRIST

"This book is a game changer and will teach you what it means to be part of This Kingdom."

Pastor Marilyn Bailey
—Teleios Church, Johannesburg,
South Africa

"There is perhaps no greater time to revisit the spiritual and practical understanding of the kingdom of God than right now.

Apostle Scantlebury addresses and corrects, common misconceptions, explains the contrasts in the Kingdom of God and the kingdom of darkness, properly aligns the Kingdom and the Church, and propels us toward a holistic understanding of Kingdom life in the earth.

With great patience and clear articulation, Apostle Scantlebury lays out a compelling case for the people of God to give priority to understanding and walking in the principles of the Kingdom of God in life and ministry.

Do yourself a favour; set aside some time to read through and study this transformative volume. You will be challenged, changed, and equipped to be a proper representative of the kingdom of God."

Apostle Eric L. Warren—Eric Warren Ministries
Charlotte, North Carolina, USA

ESCHATOLOGY – A BIBLICAL VIEW

If you were a time traveler and traveled back to the time of say Abraham Lincoln and told him you were from the future in 21st century. What if he asked you how people communicated in the 21st century, and now you had to try and explain say how an email works. How would you explain it?

Would you use something he would be familiar with to describe it? Perhaps you would tell him that in the future postmen would ride horses at 500 mile per hour. Or you might tell him you could deliver a message by train from New York to LA in less than one day. You're trying to find a way to communicate how "fast" an email really is. But you're trying to do in a way that wouldn't totally blow his mind.

That's kind of the conundrum we have when trying to understand difficult verses in the Bible, especially in themes like eschatology. The prophetic writers of Scripture had to convey God's mysteries in language that their readers would understand.

Fast forward now 2-3,000 years later, and we are reading these prophetic Scriptures through a 21st century lens, and sometimes coming up with all kinds of weird speculative interpretations because we didn't understand what those Scriptures would have meant to a first century Believer, or a Jew living in the time of the OT Prophets.

The book before you plan to delve deeper into this and much more as it seeks to present you with a sensible view of eschatology.

THE RESTORATION OF ZION

When you hear the word Zion, what comes to mind? As Christians, we've sung the choruses and the hymns about Zion or Mount Zion, but do we fully understand just what we're singing about? Do we know what it is? The Bible promises the full restoration of Zion, and if we don't fully know what Zion is, what then do we anticipate in terms of its restoration?

The greatest hindrance to accurate interpretation and application of Scripture is a futuristic view of Scripture. This futuristic view continues to rob the Believer of experiencing God in His fullness in the here and now.

In this book, we will uncover within the Scriptures exactly what Zion actually represents to the New Testament Believer. So lay down any preconceived ideas you may have, delve into the pages of this book, and let it speak truth to you.

AS IT WAS IN THE BEGINNING SO SHALL IT BE...

Have you ever wondered about life and all of its intricacies? Why are we here on planet earth? What is out there in deep dark space? Who created it all in its majesty and wonder with the brilliancy of everything that surrounds us?

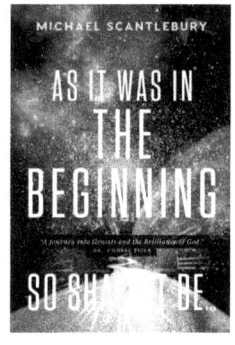

Since time began, man has tried to explain things regarding the known world. One forward thinker put forth a theory that the world was flat. That was refuted by more research. Study and research and pondering some more have revealed some truth about our world but not all the questions are yet answered.

While many of us as Christians enjoy documentaries on the pondering of the many ways we may have "gotten here" beginning with the theory of alien transports dropping us off, to the idea of a cosmic slime pit which one day came to life, so truly the only authority we have as born-again followers of Jesus Christ is the book of Genesis, the very first book of the Holy Scriptures, which simply states: "In the beginning God created the heavens and the earth." Genesis 1:1

We will broach the answers to these and other questions only God's inspired word, the Holy Bible will answer the many questions at hand.

We will begin our journey into the heart and mind of this incredible Creator to learn the reason and purpose for our existence. And as we take that incredible journey, we would seek to come to terms with the revealed, eventual outcome of our existence and life upon planet earth.

STUDY GUIDE – DANIEL IN BABYLON

This is an exciting study into the present truth lifestyle illustrated through the lives of Daniel and his friends. Whether you'll be meeting with others in a group or going through this book on your own, you've made an excellent decision by choosing to read **DANIEL in Babylon** and studying it in-depth with this guide.

This is a seminal study with strong Apostolic messaging, yet its flowing style allows for easy assimilation of biblical truths, and provides accurate insights for the cerebral Believer, who like Daniel and his companions, are usually the target of the world system. In this book various methodologies are outlined through which, spiritual Babylon seeks to entice the brightest and best of every Godly generation, to acculturize, rob of spiritual identity and manipulate to promote world kingdom end.

PRINCIPLES FOR VICTORIOUS LIVING: VOL II

The initial purpose of the five-fold ministry is for the perfecting or maturing of the Saints, which leads to its next intention, which is the real work of the ministry of Jesus Christ, reconciling the world back to the Father. This book lends itself to help in the maturing of the Saints. It adds insight and strategies that help in achieving exponential personal growth preparing one for the real work of the ministry. This is a volume of information and revelation needed in such a time as this, when maturity and focus are the needed key components that bring us an overcoming victory in this realm and advance the Kingdom of God.

PRINCIPLES FOR VICTORIOUS LIVING: VOL I

The information contained herein is well balanced with a spiritual maturity that keenly stems from wisdom and revelation in the knowledge of Christ. This is the anointing of an Apostle, and the truths that our brother shares will certainly cause you to excel in the Kingdom of God long before this life is over when later we enter the eternals. There's so much to experience today in this life, and Michael extracts so much from the Word of God to facilitate that. His insight of revelation and ability to interpret and articulate what his spirit receives from the Lord are powerful.

PRESENT TRUTH LIFESTYLE
– DANIEL IN BABYLON

This is a seminal study with strong Apostolic messaging, yet its flowing style allows for easy assimilation of biblical truths, and provides accurate insights for the cerebral Believer, who like Daniel and his companions, are usually the target of the world system. In this book various methodologies are outlined through which, spiritual Babylon seeks to entice the brightest and best of every Godly generation, to acculturize, rob of spiritual identity and manipulate to promote world kingdom end.

But thanks be to God, there is still a generation in the earth spiritually alert enough to operate within the world system, yet deploy their talents and giftings to bring honour and glory to God. Those with the Daniel mindset will decode dreams and visions and interpret judgements written on the kingdoms of this world in this season.

ESTHER PRESENT TRUTH CHURCH

In a season where the Church co-exists harmoniously with truth and error, this book provides us with a precision tool and well-calibrated instrument of change that is able to fine-tune the global Body of Christ.

The Book of Esther is rich with revelation that is still valid and applicable for the day in which we live.

Hidden within its pages is a powerful "present truth" message. The lives of the people involved and the conditions that are seen have spiritual parallels for the Church. Our destiny as the Body of Christ is revealed. The preparations and conditions we must attain to are all similar.

THE FORTRESS CHURCH

According to Webster's English Dictionary "fortress" is defined as: a fortified place: stronghold, *especially*: A large and permanent fortification sometimes including a town. A place that is protected against attack. This book seeks to describe what is a "Fortress Church". We would be looking into the dynamics of this Church as described in Jacob's vision in Genesis Chapter 28, also as described by the Prophet Isaiah, in Isaiah Chapter 2 and as the one detailed in a Psalm of the sons of Korah in Psalms Chapter 48. We would also be looking at a working model of this type of church as found at Antioch in the Book of Acts. Finally we would be exploring The Church at Ephesus, where the Apostle Paul by the Holy Spirit revealed some powerful descriptions of The Church.

CALLED TO BE AN APOSTLE

This autobiography spans fifty-two years of my life on the earth thus far and I have the hope of living several more... Our home was always packed with young people and we did enjoy times of really wonderful fellowship! Although we were experiencing these wonderful times of fellowship my appetite and desire to grow in the things of God continued unabated. I continued to read anything and everything that I could put my hands on that would strengthen my life. I began reading Wigglesworth, Moody, Finney, Idahosa, Lake, and the list went on and on! But the more I read the more this question burned in my heart–"*why is it that every time we hear/read about a move of God, it is always miles away and in another country? Why can't I experience some of the things that I am reading about?*" Little did I know the Lord would answer that desire!

LEAVENED REVEALED

The Bible has a lot to say about *leaven* and its effects upon the Believer. Leaven as an ingredient gives a false sense of growth. In the New Testament there are at least six types of *leaven* spoken about and we will be exploring them in detail, in order to ensure that our lives are completely free of the first five, and completely influenced by the sixth! These types of leaven include the following: The leaven of the Pharisees; The leaven of the Sadducees; The leaven of the Galatians; The leaven of Herod; The leaven of the Corinthians. However, the Leaven of the Kingdom of God is the only type of leaven that has the power and capacity to bring about true growth and lasting change to our lives.

I WILL BUILD MY CHURCH — JESUS CHRIST

"For we are his *masterpiece*, created in Christ Jesus for good works that God prepared long ago to be our way of life." Ephesians 2:10

What a powerful picture of The Church of Jesus Christ–His Masterpiece! Reference to a *masterpiece* lends to the idea that there are other pieces and among them all, this particular one stands head and shoulders above the rest! This is so true when it comes to The Church that Jesus Christ is building; when you place it alongside everything else that God has created, The Church is by far His Masterpiece!

JESUS CHRIST THE APOSTLE AND HIGH PRIEST OF OUR PROFESSION

There is a dimension to the apostolic nature of Jesus Christ that I would like to capture in His one-on-one encounters with several people during the time He walked the face of the earth and functioned as Apostle. In this book we will explore several significant encounters that Jesus Christ had with different people where valuable principles and insight can be gleaned. They are designed to change your life.

FIVE PILLARS OF THE APOSTOLIC

It has become very evident that a new day has dawned in the earth, as the Lord restores the foundational ministry of the Apostle back to His Church. This book will give you a clear and concise understanding of what the Holy Spirit is doing in The Church today.

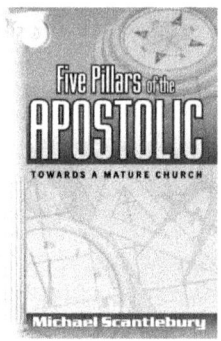

APOSTOLIC PURITY

In every dispensation, in every move of God's Holy Spirit to bring restoration and reformation to His Church, righteousness, holiness and purity has always been of utmost importance to the Lord. This book will challenge your to walk pure as you seek to fulfil God's Will for your life and ministry.

GOD'S NATURE EXPRESSED THROUGH HIS NAMES

How awesome it would be when we encounter God's Nature through the varied expressions of His Names. His Names give us reference and guidance as to how He works towards and in us as His people–and by extension to society! As a matter of fact it adds a whole new meaning to how you draw near to Him; and by this you can now begin to know His Ways because you have come into relationship with His Nature.

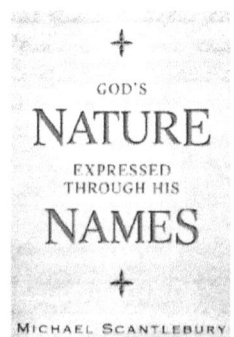

INTERNAL REFORMATION

Internal Reformation is multifaceted. It is an ecclesiology laying out the blue print of The Church Jesus Christ is building in today's world. At the same time it is a manual laying out the modus operandi of how Believers are called to function as dynamic, militant over-comers who are powerful because they carry internally the very character and DNA of Jesus Christ.

KINGDOM ADVANCING PRAYER VOL I

The Church of Jesus Christ is stronger and much more determined and equipped than she has ever been, and strong, aggressive, powerful, Spirit-Filled, Kingdom-centred prayers are being lifted in every nation in the earth. This kind of prayer is released from the heart of Father God into the hearts of His people, as we seek for His Glory to cover the earth as the waters cover the sea.

APOSTOLIC REFORMATION

If the axe is dull, And one does not sharpen the edge, Then he must use more strength; But wisdom brings success." (Ecclesiastes 10:10) For centuries The Church of Jesus Christ has been using quite a bit of strength while working with a dull axe (sword, Word of God, revelation), in trying to get the job done. This has been largely due to the fact that she has been functioning without Apostles, the ones who have been graced and anointed by the Lord, with the ability to sharpen.

KINGDOM ADVANCING PRAYER VOL II

Prayer is calling for the Bridegroom's return, and for the Bride to be made ready. Prayers are storming the heavens and binding the "strong men" declaring and decreeing God's Kingdom rule in every jurisdiction. This is what we call Kingdom Advancing Prayer. What a *Glorious Day* to be *Alive* and to be in the *Will* and *Plan of Father God*! *Hallelujah*!

KINGDOM ADVANCING PRAYER VOLUME III

One of the keys to the amazing rise to greater functionality of The Church is the clear understanding of what we call Kingdom Advancing Prayer. This kind of prayer reaches into the very core of the demonic stronghold and destroys demonic kings and princes and establishes the Kingdom and Purpose of the Lord. This is the kind of prayer that Jesus Christ engaged in, to bring to pass the will of His Father while He was upon planet earth.